MW01025736

TWILIGHT ANOINTING
PRAYER BOOK

*Introduction to Spiritual Warfare
and Biblical Principles*

Bernice Gibbs

WESTBOW
PRESS
A DIVISION OF THOMAS NELSON

WestBow Press books may be ordered through booksellers or by contacting:

WestBow Press
A Division of Thomas Nelson
1663 Liberty Drive
Bloomington, IN 47403
www.westbowpress.com
1-(866) 928-1240

ISBN: 978-1-4497-5944-5 (sc)
ISBN: 978-1-4497-5943-8 (hc)
ISBN: 978-1-4497-5945-2 (e)

Library of Congress Control Number: 2012912376

Printed in the United States of America

WestBow Press rev. date: 09/28/2012

CONTENTS

INTRODUCTION

Satan, I declare to you in the name of Jesus that you have no authority over the readers of this book according to Matthew 18:18. I bind you from operating against them in any way. Their lives are hidden in Christ. Satan, you have no power to bring any part of the curse upon the readers. I take my stand as a believer and we take our place in Christ.

Now Father, we worship you. We give you reverence. We confess with our mouth that your word will not return to you void. We praise you for your protection and for your goodness upon our lives. We thank you that Satan is unable to penetrate that. Thank you for bringing total healing, deliverance, and completion to the readers of these prayers. Jeremiah 33:3 states "Call to me and I will answer you and tell you great and unsearchable things you do not know."

THE PURPOSES OF PRAYER

Prayer <u>moves the hand</u> of God to work in the affairs of men
Exodus 3:7 Acts 12:5 Jonah 2:1

Prayer <u>keeps us</u> spiritually fit and alert
Matthew 26:41 1 Peter 4:7

Prayer <u>transforms us</u> into the image of Christ
Luke 9:28-29

Prayer <u>unleashes</u> the power and blessings of God

Acts 2:1 Acts 4:23-31

Prayer is God's <u>means of obtaining</u> our material and spiritual desires

Matthew 7:7-8 John 14:13-14 John 16:23-24

Prayer and faith is like a combination lock. It blows open an array of heavenly blessings that Jesus is waiting, with much love, to give to whosoever will go after it.

Mark 11:24, "Therefore I tell you, whatever you ask for in prayer, believe that you have received it, and it will be yours." NIV

Confronting the Devil's Tactics

Many of these warfare prayers are taken from the book of Psalms. David's prophetic prayers were weapons against the enemy's attempt to stop the promised seed. David's struggles were with natural enemies but behind these natural enemies were spiritual ones that were opposed to the Davidic kingdom. David's victories in prayer opened the way for his throne to continue.

Jesus was to come from this lineage and sit upon this throne. David was fighting something beyond the natural. Through the Holy Spirit, he was contending with the powers of darkness that were set against the arrival of the kingdom of God. That throne of wickedness was unable to overcome the throne of righteousness. These powers were also manifested through Herod, who attempted to kill the coming Messiah. Herod was driven by spirits of fear and murder.

The Holy Spirit had already been loosed through the prayers of David and because of his prayers, David's throne was secure. God taught David and he became a warrior king. His victories caused his kingdom to be established. His victory over the house of Saul came after a long war. 2 Samuel 3:1 states "Now there was a long war between the house of Saul and the house of David.

But David grew stronger and stronger, and the house of Saul grew weaker and weaker". David consumed his enemies and he did not turn until they were destroyed. (Psalm 18:37)

Do not allow the enemy to strategize against you. Overcome and destroy Satan's strategies through prayer. Ephesians 6:11 tells us to put on the whole armor of God that we may be able to stand against the wiles, (tricks or traps) of the Devil. David prayed for his enemies to be scattered, confused, exposed, and destroyed.

THE BLOOD OF JESUS AS A WEAPON

The blood will paralyze and cut off the head of your enemy. Let the blood of the cross stand between you and any dark power that be delegated against family, church, and community. I believe that life and death are in your tongue.

I eat with the heart of faith and the flesh of Jesus, for it is written "His flesh is bread indeed; I eat it now so that I can also eat with Him in His glory".

Leviticus 17:11 states, "For the life of the flesh is in the blood, and I have given it to you upon the altar to make atonement for your souls; for it *is* the blood *that* makes atonement for the soul."

The blood of Jesus contains the life of Jesus. I eat the flesh of Jesus to receive new spiritual strength, strength to paralyze the desires of my flesh, and vigor to paralyze the power of my flesh and make it obedient to the laws of the Lord. I apply the blood of Jesus by decrees and confessions.

Hebrews 12:24, "To Jesus the mediator of the new covenant and to the blood of sprinkling that speaks better things than that of Abel."

The blood of Jesus brings life to you, your family, and loved ones. The blood of Jesus can speak destruction to your enemies and bring healing to your body.

♦For it is written, life is in the blood, and as I eat and drink the flesh and blood of my Lord Jesus Christ, I receive into myself the virtues, strength, power, might, and anointing in the blood. I let the blood re-energize, revitalize, reactivate, and revise all dead potential and spiritual gifts within me.

♦Let the blood flush out all evil deposits from my system and let the blood clean my spiritual vision and wash all of my spiritual pipes that I may receive of the Lord unhindered blessings. I possess the life and the Spirit of Christ within me.

♦I believe in the unshakeable and eternal power in the Word of God. The blood of Jesus can never lose its power because it is a divine blood.

John 1:14, "And the Word became flesh and dwelt among us, and we beheld His glory, the glory as of the only begotten of the Father, full of grace and truth."

Revelation 12:11, "And they overcame him by the blood of the Lamb and by the word of their testimony, and they did not love their lives to the death."

♦Let the Word of God raise up in me every down trodden area of my life. Lord, make me drunken with your blood and strengthen me with your might; I soak myself in the blood of Jesus. Heavenly Father, it is written that I shall be strong in you and in the power of your might. Gird me with all your strength and let me not fall into the trench or pit of my enemies, Hallelujah!

♦I draw a circle of the blood of Jesus around me, my family, my church, my property, and finances in Jesus' name.

♦I overcome you, Devil, by the blood of the Lamb.

♦Let the blood of Jesus speak disappearance into every infirmity in my life, in the name of Jesus.

♦Let the blood of Jesus dry up every evil tree used against me and anyone connected to me in the name of Jesus.

♦I apply the blood of Jesus to demonic, satanic spirits: you cannot enter my house.

♦I sprinkle the blood of Jesus on all that is released to me.

♦You cannot put any sickness on me, because I am redeemed by the blood of the Lamb.

♦I speak peace into every broken marriage; let the blood of Jesus minister defeat to every evil work in our lives.

♦I speak the blood of Jesus into the enemy's camp and confuse them.

♦I hold the blood of Jesus against the spirit of stagnation in any area of my life, my children's lives, and the church in the name of Jesus.

♦I hold the blood of Jesus against every delayed and denied promotion.

♦I hold the blood of Jesus against dead, half-empty accounts.

♦I create a boundary against you, Devil, by the blood of Jesus Christ.

♦I speak the blood of Jesus against the demonic and satanic delay of my miracles.

♦I hold the blood of Jesus against lack of good helpers in my home and church.

◆I call death unto the enemy who holds the progress in my life by the blood of Jesus.

ALL IN THE NAME

John 14:13-14: "Whatever you ask [demand] in my name, I [Jesus] will do it."

Then Peter said "In the name of Jesus Christ of Nazareth, rise up and walk." He asked or (demanded) that the man get up and walk in the name of Jesus, according to Acts 3.

Ephesians 5:20, "Giving thanks always for all things to God the Father in the name of our Lord Jesus Christ"

Acts 16:16-18, "Now it happened, as we went to prayer, that a certain slave girl possessed with a spirit of divination met us, who brought her masters much profit by fortune-telling. This girl followed Paul and us, and cried out, saying, "These men are the servants of the Most High God, who proclaim to us the way of salvation." And this she did for many days.

But Paul, greatly annoyed, turned and said to the spirit, "I command you in the name of Jesus Christ to come out of her." And he came out that very hour.

Paul cast a demon out of a possessed girl in the name of Jesus. This set her free and stirred the city of Ephesus to its very foundation. He commanded the demon, in the name of Jesus Christ, to come out of her and he came out the same hour.

Paul did not speak to the girl, he spoke to the spirit. The spirit had to come out; no possibility existed of its not doing so. Philippians

2:9-10 states "Therefore God also has highly exalted Him and given Him the name which is above every name, that at the name of Jesus every knee should bow, of those in heaven, and of those on earth, and of those under the earth". That spirit had to bow to the name of Jesus. What a treasure we have in the name of Jesus, and yet, we have neglected it.

Do not deal with the person; Jesus said deal with the spirit. There is no distance in the realm of the spirit. The Lord said, to simply, speak to that spirit and command him to come out in His name. There is power in the name of Jesus.

Ephesians 6:12, "For we do not wrestle against flesh and blood, but against principalities, against powers, against the rulers of the darkness of this age, against spiritual hosts of wickedness in the heavenly places."

The power to conquer is in the name of Jesus of Nazareth, the Son of the Living God! Hallelujah!!!

Confession

The name of Jesus belongs to me. Satan, you are a defeated foe. I am no longer afraid of you. You were my master and I was your slave. But now I am your master because Jesus made me master over all evil powers and all demons. I am free in the name of Jesus. I have authority over demons. In the name of Jesus, Satan, I break your power over my family, my church, my spirit, my soul, and my body. Everything is subject to the name of Jesus. For every knee (of things or beings) shall bow, in Heaven and in Earth. Amen

God gave Him (Jesus) a name above every name! that name belongs to me. There is power in that name. There is majesty in that name. There is authority in that name. There is glory in that name. Hallelujah. Amen!

He is:

- Lord of Lords Psalm136:3
- Son of David Matt 1:1
- The Shadow of the Almighty Ps. 91:1
- My strong refuge Ps. 71:7
- My Rock, my strong tower Ps.31:2 Prov 18:10
- A sure foundation Isaiah 28:16
- My sweet smelling savor Eph. 5:2
- My strength Isaiah 12:2
- King of Kings
- Wonderful Counselor Isaiah 9:6
- A Very Present help in trouble Ps. 46:1
- The True Vine John 15:5
- The True Bread from Heaven
- The well of Living Water John 4:14
- Wall of Holy Fire Zechariah 2:5
- A Star out of Jacob Numbers 24:17
- A stone cut out of the Mountain Daniel 2:45
- The Light of the World
- The Way the Truth and the light
- Him that Sitteth on the Throne
- He who Hath Seven Spirits of God
- He who satisfies thy mouth with good things
- My Cup
- Horn of my Salvation
- The Portion of my Inheritance
- The Lord Strong and Mighty
- The Lord mighty in Battle
- The King of Glory
- The Lord of Hosts
- My Help and my Deliverer
- My Hiding Place

- Father of the Fatherless
- The God of Abraham
- The Most High God
- The Lord, our Maker
- God of Longsuffering
- Who forgives all your iniquities
- Everlasting God
- The Faithful God
- Almighty God
- The Lord God of Elijah

DELIVERANCE FROM SUBSTANCE ABUSE AND ALCOHOL

- Heavenly Father, I pray that you give me (him/her) the strength to resist drugs. James 4:7

- I bind every evil strategy the enemy has planned to keep me (him/her) in this addiction in the name of Jesus. I plead the Blood of Jesus over my (his/her) body. God has plans for good and not evil. Jeremiah 29:11

- O Lord, with each new day, help me (him/her) to be strong and continue to trust you in Jesus' name.

- Heavenly Father, bring into my (his/her) eyes and heart, an honesty that sees the true situation and find strength that I can change in the name of Jesus.

◆Heavenly Father, cleanse my (his/her) mind of all darkness; fill it with love and light. Almighty God, you sent Jesus to set the captives free. Isaiah 61

◆Lord, I know you can deliver me (him/her) from all addictions and bondages that have kept me (him/her) from being and doing better.

◆Heavenly Father, I ask that you send your angelic warriors to drive back the stronghold of addiction in the name of Jesus. God, you get all the glory. Amen.

◆I break the demonic spirit of selling drugs in the name of Jesus.

◆Lord I (he/she) seek your face asking that you would empower me (him/her) with your strength. Strengthen my (his/her) mind, heart, and will to resist the cravings, desires, and needs for drugs. Thank you Heavenly Father.

◆I speak your word that I am more than a conqueror through Jesus Christ.

◆Father, I thank you for giving me (him/her) power, strength, and a mind to overcome this alcohol and drug addiction.

◆Heavenly Father, cause the high and intoxication I (he/she) gets from the drugs to no longer be effective upon the mind and body; cause the taste I (he/she) get from taking them become nasty and undesirable in the name of Jesus.

◆I (he/she) am indeed set free from the snare and the bondage of this drug addiction from Satan. I command you to loose your stronghold from my (his/her) life now in Jesus name.

◆I break the power of incarceration from me (him/her) now, in the name of Jesus.

◆Satan, I break your yoke of bondage that has enslaved me (him/her) to drugs.

◆Satan, I render you helpless, powerless, inoperative, and ineffective to draw, control, or manipulate me (him/her) to drugs by power and authority in the name of Jesus.

◆I declare this body is temple of the Holy Ghost.

◆I prayed in confidence that my (his/her) eyes are open to see and go to a kingly place, wear the best robe, best ring, eat the best food, and possess the best life. Thank you Heavenly Father.

PRAYING THE SCRIPTURES

Scripture prayer links time and eternity. Prayer is the communication bridge that links Heaven and Earth. It allows time to pierce into eternity. Praying the scriptures illuminate God's will, ignites prayer, and outlasts time.

Psalm 119:105, 130
[105] Your word is a lamp to my feet
And a light to my path.
[130] The entrance of Your words gives light; It gives understanding to the simple.

Habakkuk 3:17-19
[17] Though the fig tree may not blossom,
Nor fruit be on the vines;
Though the labor of the olive may fail,
And the fields yield no food;
Though the flock may be cut off from the fold,

And there be no herd in the stalls—
[18] Yet I will rejoice in the Lord,
I will joy in the God of my salvation.
[19] The Lord God[a] is my strength;
He will make my feet like deer's *feet,*
And He will make me walk on my high hills.

Psalms 19:8
The statutes of the Lord are right, rejoicing the heart;
The commandment of the Lord is pure, enlightening the eyes;

Philippians 4:7-8
[7] And the peace of God, which surpasses all understanding, will guard your hearts and minds through Christ Jesus. [8] Finally, brethren, whatever things are true, whatever things are noble, whatever things are just, whatever things are pure, whatever things are lovely, whatever things are of good report, if there is any virtue and if there is anything praiseworthy—meditate on these things.

Psalms 103:1-3
Bless the Lord, O my soul;
And all that is within me, bless His holy name!
[2] Bless the Lord, O my soul,
And forget not all His benefits:
[3] Who forgives all your iniquities,
Who heals all your diseases,

Psalm 23:1-4 The Message Bible
[1-3] God, my shepherd! I don't need a thing. You have bedded me down in lush meadows; you find me quiet pools to drink from. True to your word, you let me catch my breath and send me in the right direction.

[4] Even when the way goes through
Death Valley,

I'm not afraid
when you walk at my side.
Your trusty shepherd's crook
makes me feel secure.

To defeat worry and fear confess these gospel pills three times a day.

I John 4:4 The Message Bible
My dear children, you come from God and belong to God. You have already won a big victory over those false teachers, for the Spirit in you is far stronger than anything in the world.

Isaiah 54:14
In righteousness you shall be established;
You shall be far from oppression, for you shall not fear;
And from terror, for it shall not come near you.

Isaiah 54:17
No weapon formed against me shall prosper, for my righteousness is of the Lord. But what even I do will prosper for I'm like a tree that's planted by the rivers of water.

Psalm 1:3
But what even I do will prosper for I'm like a tree that's planted by the rivers of water.

James 4:7
Therefore submit to God. Resist the devil and he will flee from you.

♦The devil flees from me because I resist him in the name of Jesus.

Psalms 119:89
Your word, O Lord is forever settled in Heaven. Therefore, I establish His word upon this earth.

Isaiah 54:13
All your children shall be taught by the Lord,
And great shall be the peace of your children.

CLEANSING HOME PRAYER

◆I renounce all opportunities and foreground, held by Satan's wicked demons, in relation to my (our) home and property. I bind, with chains and fetters, all wicked spirits along with their schemes and assignments against this home and property.

◆I ask you Lord, Jesus Christ, to evict any controlling power of darkness from my home and property. I send them to where they can never control or harm any person again by the power of Jesus' Blood.

◆Heavenly Father, in the name of Jesus, I now renounce all past use of this property for occult practices, magic, sorcery, witchcraft, divination, false religions, curses, spells, hexes, satanic spells, voodoo spells, and spiritualistic healings. I apply the blood of Jesus.

◆I remove and declare that all wicked works, tentacles, roots, fruits, links, and spirits be forced out to where Jesus sends you. I loose God's presence in this home and on this property.

◆I ask you Lord to loose your angels in great abundance in my home, my property, and my presence to protect us, to guard us, to force, and to drive out all demonic spirits. They cannot return to me again.

•Heavenly Father, I ask you to create a hedge of protection around us and keep our minds sound in the name of Jesus.

•I loose the mighty, warring angels around each of us. Heavenly Father, I apply the blood of Jesus over the doorways. I ask that the enemy be rendered powerless and harmless so they cannot comeback through these doorways ever again to our property, our home, our finances, our children, our ministries, and our work places, in the name of Jesus. Hallelujah!

•I blind the enemy's eyes so that he cannot see. I bind the enemy's ears so that he cannot hear. I bind them and command them not to manifest in my presence. I apply the Blood of Jesus over each of us and the airway that surrounds us.

PRAYER BINDING AND LOOSING DEMONIC SPIRITS

•In the name of the Lord Jesus Christ of Nazareth, I bind all of Satan's evil, wicked, demonic, lying, and tormenting spirits. I bind the strongmen along with all evil principalities, powers, and rulers of wickedness in high places, roots, fruits, tentacles, and links including , strongmen of doubt, unbelief, leviathan, pride, anger, rage, strife, deception, self-deception, confusion, self-confusion, divination, Jezebel, python, familiar spirits, delusions, belittling, and bitterness.

•I loose all foul, demonic spirits and strongmen from every organ and cell in my body. I loose these spirits from every gland, muscle, ligament, and bone in my body. I loose these spirits from my home, my properties, my marriage, my car, my church, my business, my ministries, my vision, my workplace, and my finances. I loose them to go where Jesus sends them. I bind them and command them to stay there in the name of Jesus Christ of Nazareth. I place the blood of the Lord Jesus Christ between me and these spirits.

(Lay your hand on yourself, anoint yourself with oil)

◆I cast down and shatter every demonic stronghold in my mind. I ask you Heavenly Father to pull down every high thought in me that exalts itself against the knowledge of God. I cast them aside, in the name of the Lord Jesus Christ of Nazareth, and bring every thought captive to the obedience of Christ Jesus, according to 2 Corinthians 10:3-6. I cast aside and destroy any demonic strongholds that are in me, or anyone that I am divinely connected with or have prayed for.

◆I ask you father to destroy them now, according to John 14:14 in the name of the Lord Jesus Christ of Nazareth. Hallelujah, to God be the glory. Amen.

◆I command my mind and my desires; my will, my emotions, my ego, my imaginations, and my thoughts, to come now to the obedience of Christ. Lord, I ask you to destroy and remove all vain imaginations, demonic strongholds, and any deceptions that are in my mind and thoughts. I cast them aside in the name of Jesus Christ.

◆Heavenly Father, wash my mind clean with the precious blood of Jesus Christ. Enable me to stay in your presence all day long according to your word. Lord your word says that your anointing oil destroys the yoke of bondage (Isaiah 10:27).

◆Heavenly Father, I ask you to cause your anointing to break and destroy any yokes of bondages along with all of their works, roots, fruits, tentacles, and links that are in my life and anyone I am connected with in the name of the Lord Jesus Christ!

BLESSINGS

Heavenly Father, your Word states in John 14:13-14, "whatever you ask in My name, that I will do, that the Father may be glorified in the Son. If you ask anything in My name, I will do it." Lord, I ask you to cover me with your anointing, your glory, and your presence.

Give me (us) a new release and a fresh flow in my inner man with rivers of living waters, springing forth abundantly with life. Fill me to overflowing with your favor, your compassion, your love, your wisdom and your understanding. Fill us with your gifts, the anointing, and the blessings that you have for me. Anoint me (us), pour your anointing on me. **[apply anointing oil to your body]**.

I receive your presence and the anointing in the name of the Father, the Son, and the Holy Spirit. I hear your voice Lord and no other voice I will follow. I ask you to expand in me your territories. Thank you, Lord, for blessing me.

THANK YOU FOR YOUR PROMISE

Heavenly Father, I come to you with a heart of thanksgiving. I thank you in all the good and the bad things because all things work for my good. You are the creator. Heavenly Father, I thank you for in your presence. And because of your presence, I have fullness of joy.

◆I am complete and whole in you. Thank you for the plan that I might have a full life, abundant and overflowing. I thank you for your provisions and that all my needs are met according to your riches in glory. I prosper in every area of my life and my soul prospers. I thank you for protection and for the peace that passes all understanding.

◆Father, I thank you that we can dwell in the secret place of the Most High. I thank you that we can abide under the shadow of our almighty God according to Psalm 91.

◆I thank you that I (we) can say that you are our Lord, our refuge, our fortress, and our God whom we can trust. Father, I thank you for delivering us from the snare of the fowler and from the deadly pestilence.

◆Father, I thank you for covering me (us) with your feathers. I thank you that I can walk under your wings and take refuge. I thank you that your faithfulness and truth is our shield and armor.

◆Heavenly Father, I am not afraid of the terror by night or for the arrow that flieth by day, nor for the pestilence that walketh in darkness, nor for the destruction that wasteth at noonday.

◆I thank you, Heavenly Father that a thousand shall fall at our side and ten thousand at our right hand and none will come near me. I thank you for giving your angels charge over me (us) to keep us in all ways and angel's hands will lift me up so I (we) do dash our foot against a stone. I can tread upon the lion and serpent and trample the young lion and the dragons under my (our) feet.

◆Father I am grateful that when I call upon you, you will answer and be with me in the time of trouble. You will deliver me and satisfy me with long life and show me your salvations.

♦Father, I thank you for spoiling all principalities and powers and making a show of them openly, triumphing over all. I claim victory for my life. I reject all the temptation and accusations of Satan.

♦I affirm that the Word of God is true and I choose to live in obedience to you, Jesus and in true fellowship with you. Thank you Father for opening my eyes and showing me those areas of my life that is not pleasing to you. Work in me to cleanse me from all ground that would give Satan a foothold against me.

♦Heavenly Father, I place all of my cares, all of my anxieties, all of my worries, and all of my concerns once and for all on you. I know you love me and watch over me according to these scriptures.

Isaiah 62:7
And give Him no rest till He establishes
And till He makes Jerusalem a praise in the earth.

Psalm 122:6
Pray for the peace of Jerusalem:
"May they prosper who love you.

1 Peter 5:7
"casting all your care upon Him, for He cares for you."

EIGHT DAY PRAYER

♦I command the morning to take hold of the ends of the earth and shake the wicked out of it. Job 38:12-13

♦I am riding on the wings of the morning into a new day of victory.

◆Every power on assignment, to reduce and diminish, the power of God in my life, die in the name of Jesus.

◆Holy Ghost fire, consume every impurity in my life that hinders me from being an effectual believer (intercessor), in the name of Jesus.

◆Love for others and love for Kingdom growth, fall afresh on me, in the name of Jesus.

◆I speak to wombs of the morning and declare and decree my day.

◆Fresh fire from heaven, fill me again and again to the brim for effectual ministry, in the name of Jesus.

◆Every scale over my eyes, fall down and die, in the name of Jesus.

◆Every stopper blocking my ears, melt away by fire, in the name of Jesus.

◆Every veil over my mind catches fire now, in the name of Jesus.

◆O Lord my God, grant me seeing eyes and hearing ears, in the name of Jesus.

◆Power to travail in love for the divine needs of others fall upon me now, in the name of Jesus.

◆Power to prevail at the altar of effectual prayers, fall upon me now in the name of Jesus.

◆I speak to wind of the morning to carry this message: I am healed through the Blood of Jesus.

◆I decree and declare a new season and a fresh anointing upon my house in the name of Jesus.

◆Every satanic cobweb spun to hinder me from the altar of intercession or church, catch fire in the name of Jesus.

◆Heavenly carpenters! Let your hammer of fire, fall upon every horn of wickedness bowing down the head of God's people in shame, in Jesus' name.

◆Lord let the grace to finish the race and finish well, fall upon me in the name of Jesus.

◆I send a message to Satan on the wings of the wind: you are bound. God's church has already won! There will be no new beginnings or new births. I declare Satan's womb barren and the Blood of Jesus is against you now!

◆Lord, lay your hand of fire upon my memory and give me a retentive memory in Jesus name.

◆I will find favor before all panels in the name of Jesus.

◆Heavenly Father, anoint my handiwork for success in the name of Jesus.

◆Let every blessing, confiscated by witchcraft and familiar spirits, be released in the name of Jesus.

◆Anointing of the overcomer, fall upon me in the name of Jesus.

◆I claim divine wisdom to answer any questions directed at me in competition.

SPIRITUAL WARFARE-FINANCE

In any situation you may find yourself in, you must remember that God is faithful to see you through it. Psalm 34:19, (NIV) "A righteous man may have many troubles but the Lord delivers him from them all". God says that you can apply your faith to see your daily needs met, Praise the Lord

•The Spirit of impossibility, loose your grip from over my life in the name of Jesus.

•My hands, in a famine land, receive power to prosper in the name of Jesus. Genesis 26:3.

•The inheritances of sinners are stored up for the just. Therefore let men bless me everywhere I go.

•I call death to poverty in my life, in the name of Jesus.

•I agree with God's word, I am living in a Godly land.

•I decree a full recovery in my business_____

Psalm 56:9, "When I cry out to you, Then my enemies will turn back; This I know, because God is for me."

Psalm 32:8, "I will instruct you and teach you in the way you should go; I will guide you with My eye."

Psalm 23:1, 6, "The Lord is my shepherd; I shall not want." "Surely goodness and mercy shall follow me all the days of my life; and I will dwell in the house of the Lord forever."

Exodus 23:20, "Behold I send an Angel before you to keep you in the way and to bring into the place which I have prepared."

•I retrieve my blessings from every evil attack in Jesus name.

•I break every curse of failure in my life and in the lives of my family members, in the name of Jesus.

•Let all monies pass under the rod to me, in the name of Jesus.

•No devourer shall destroy the fruit of my labor. Hallelujah!

•I shall dwell in prosperity; my descendants shall inherit the earth.

•I trust in the Lord and do good, dwelling in a prosperous and blessed land, AMEN.

◆God's ears are open to my cry. The eyes of the Lord are on the righteous.

◆I shall never be moved in my prosperity, in the name of Jesus.

◆I apply the blood of Jesus over our business and jobs.

◆I apply the blood of Jesus over our finances and our possessions.

◆I apply the blood Jesus over our bills, our checking and savings account.

◆I apply the blood of Jesus over our home, door posts, and windows according to Exodus 12:7.

◆I apply the blood of Jesus over our cloud of witnesses for us wherever we go.

◆I declare and decree that where the blood of Jesus Christ is applied, Satan can't enter according to Hebrews 10:4-23.
I confess now that Jesus is Lord over my family, my church, and my finances.

Pray in the spirit now according to Romans 8:26

SPIRITUAL WARFARE-FINANCE

Deuteronomy 8:18, "But thou shall remember the LORD thy God: for it is he that giveth thee power to get wealth, that he may establish his covenant which he swear unto thy fathers, as it is this day."

3 John 2, "Beloved, I wish above all things that thou mayest prosper and be in health, even as thy soul prosperity."

Job 36:11 states "If they obey and serve him, they shall spend their days in prosperity, and their years in pleasures."

Psalm 84:11-12, "For the LORD God is a sun and shield: the LORD will give grace and glory: no good thing will he withhold from them that walk uprightly. [12]O LORD of hosts, blessed is the man that trusteth in thee."

♦I remove my name and those of my family or my customers from the book of financial bankruptcy in Jesus' name.

♦My business brings prosperity in the name of Jesus.

♦I declare that Satan will have no control over my finances, in Jesus name.

♦Let the ministering spirit (God's Angels) go forth and bring in blessings unto me in the name of Jesus.

♦The Lord rebukes the devourer for my sake. No weapon that is formed against me will prosper.

♦All obstacles and hindrances to my prosperity are now dissolved.

♦God has given me all things that pertain to life and godliness and I am well able to possess all that God had provided for me 2 Peter 1:3-4.

Praise & Worship GOD NOW

MIDNIGHT BATTLE

♦I release the warring angels of God to scatter those who are plotting against me and my destiny, in the name of Jesus.

◆Every demonic python and dragon, working against my life and my family's lives; I speak to the air and the water that they breathe to dry up now, in the name of Jesus.

◆Holy Ghost, arise and link me with those who will bless me in the name of Jesus.

◆Holy Spirit, place the right person or people in my pathway that will lead me into divine connection spiritually and physically, in the name of Jesus.

◆O God of Elijah arise and disappoint my marital enemies, in the name of Jesus.

◆My Father, change the rule for my sake like Ephraim (cross your hands in my favor) in the name of Jesus.

◆O Lord, breathe upon me by your glory, in the name of Jesus.

◆I cut off the ministry of Judas Iscariot from my finances, in the name of Jesus.

◆Every sickness, refusing to let me go, receives double destruction in the name of Jesus. The blood of Jesus is against you Satan.

◆I decree my finances, my health, and my family are made whole, now in the Jesus name.

◆I decree every demonic spirit covering our community to dry up, now in Jesus name.

◆Every generation of financial debt is broken and dismantled in the name of Jesus.

◆Holy Ghost fire, destroy and burn to ashes, any alter of affliction raised against me and my family, in the mighty name of Jesus.

The 11th hour may appear in my situation, but there is a change taking place at 12:01. Hallelujah!

SPIRITUAL WARFARE

♦I release me from the sin and curse of my paternal and maternal families up to eight generations in the mighty name of Jesus.

♦I command every territorial alter, marine alter, and astral alter raised against my life, to collapse now in Jesus mighty name.

♦Almighty Father, I use the blood of Jesus to erase all invisible satanic labels, marks or sign from any part of my spirit, soul and body, in the name of Jesus.

I declare: From this day forward goodness and mercies, greatness and favor, sign and wonders shall continue to follow me all the days of my life and I shall dwell in the presence of the Lord forever in Jesus mighty name.

I decree: I will climb upon your high places I will be celebrated among princes and princesses of the land; I will make an impact wherever I go. Though my beginning may be small my latter end will greatly increase.

Your testimony will go far and near; it will tingle the ears of men. They shall inquire after it, and they shall say of you, the Lord had been very good to you. So shall it be for you and yours in Jesus name.

Psalm 65:11-13, "Thou crownest the year with thy goodness; and thy paths drop fatness. [12]They drop upon the pastures of the wilderness: and the little hills rejoice on every side. [13]The pastures are clothed with flocks; the valleys also are covered over with corn; they shout for joy, they also sing."

Matthew 20:16, "So the last shall be first, and the first last."

Psalm 102:13, "Thou shalt arise, and have mercy upon Zion: for the time to favors her, yea, the set time, is come."

POWER OVER DEATH

1 Corinthians 15:55
"O Death, where is your sting?
O Hades, where is your victory?"

Hebrews 5:7 (NIV)
"During the days of Jesus' life on earth, he offered up prayers and petitions with loud cries and tears to the one who could save him from death, and he was heard because of his reverent submission"

Psalm 118:17
"I will not die but live, and proclaim what the Lord has done."

Psalm 91:16 NIV
"With long life I will satisfy him and show him my salvation"

Death was defeated the day Jesus rose from the dead. Resurrection morning marked the defeat of the devil. I shall not die but live and declare the works of God. God has promised that he will satisfy us with long life. I break and loose myself from any spiritual agreement that the devil set for death. Satan, you won't use my life for promotion.

I close every door opened to Satan that will bring death. I break and loose myself and my loved ones from every dark spirit and satanic bondage that brings death to my life. Every poison comes out of my life and my body now. Lord, drain sickness and worry out of my life. I destroy all secret power sources that hinder me. Every tentacle and root of death, I tear it down and destroy the hidden works of the enemy.

Rebuke the spirit of death using these prayer points and fulfill the number of your days. Pray these prayers and you shall have the last laugh and God will perfect that which concerns you.

•Let my prayer alters receive power today in the name of Jesus.

•Lord let your glory be manifested in my life in the name of Jesus.

•I break and loose myself from any curse, bewitching, witchcraft, and charm put upon my life and the lives of my family, in the name of Jesus.

•I overthrow and release myself from evil demonic control in the name of Jesus.

•I break any evil stronghold of death over my life and my spouse's life.

•Every power, speaking impossibility into my present unfavorable situation, fall down and die from the root in the name of Jesus.

•Blood of Jesus flush out and scatter witchcraft meetings summoned for my sake. I seal and rebuke it with the blood.

•I bind and cast out any spirit executing evil curses against me in the name of Jesus.

•Let the blood of Jesus rub off evil ointment upon my head I call goodness upon my body in the name of Jesus.

•Every visible and invisible alter, I sentence it to confusion and trouble all year in the name of Jesus.

•Let the river of cancer, in my family line, flowing into my life dry up from the roots and never return in the name of Jesus.

◆I speak failure into every satanic weapon formed against my life, my spouse's life, and my children in the name of Jesus.

◆Every agent of health destruction working in my life fall and die now by the blood of Jesus.

◆I speak frustration into every evil snare and satanic pit fashioned against my family, my church, and my life in the name of Jesus.

◆Let favor meet favor in my life and be mightily increased in the name of Jesus.

◆I terminate every evil progress of death in every area of my life in the name of Jesus.

◆I will become all that God created me to be in the name of Jesus.

◆I cancel reports brought against me and my spouse in the kingdom of darkness in the name of Jesus.

◆I revoke and nullify every judgment passed upon me in the kingdom of darkness in the name of Jesus.

◆I abort the operation and assignment of the power of darkness commissioned against my name, my family, and my church in the name of Jesus.

You Are Sentenced To Win

Every born again child of God has been sentenced to victory. Why don't we believe that we have what God says we can have? Is it so hard to have faith that we are who God says we are?

Confession

◆I will wait upon the Lord and he shall renew my strength. I shall mount up with wings as eagles.

♦I shall run and not be weary. I shall walk and not faint.

♦I am His workmanship created in Christ Jesus unto good works.

♦God's creation is always good! God has never created a failure.

♦Jesus became poor that I might become rich.

♦I place the cross of Jesus between me and Satan.

♦I forbid you to never return or deposit any other evil thing in the name of Jesus.

♦I speak destruction to the fruit of [satanic time table], infirmities, circle of problems, miracle delayers, closed roads, parental curses, incomplete victories, luke-warmness in prayer, drug dependence, lack of direction, rejection, anger, debts, false vision, overeating, enchantment, marital downgrading, caged finances, satanic syringes, examination failure, and failure of divine promise.

♦Any demons living inside any member of my body or household depart now in the name of Jesus.

♦Every spirit of pocket with holes is mended by the blood of Jesus.

♦Let my prayers release angelic intervention to my favor in the name of Jesus.

♦I destroy the walls of security around my enemies in the name of Jesus.

♦My heavens shall not become brass.

♦Let all stubborn demons be strangled to death.

♦Let the fire of God begin to melt every evil resistance to my progress

♦From the north, south, east, and west, I claim all my blessings now in the name of Jesus.

♦Let the hammer of the almighty God smash and shatter every evil alter erected against me in the name of Jesus.

♦Holy Ghost, refill me that I might bring forth good fruit.

♦Every evil priest ministering against me at the evil alter receive the sword of God in the mouth, eyes, and ears in the name of Jesus.

♦Any hand that wants to retaliate or arrest me because of all these prayers, dry up and wither to the root, in the name of Jesus. My prayers will not return back void. Hallelujah!

ENCOURAGEMENT

I decree joy and happiness in my life, in the name of Jesus

Philippians 4:6-8

[6] Be anxious for nothing, but in everything by prayer and supplication, with thanksgiving, let your requests be made known to God; [7] and the peace of God, which surpasses all understanding, will guard your hearts and minds through Christ Jesus. [8] Finally, brethren, whatever things are true, whatever things are noble, whatever things are just, whatever things are pure, whatever things are lovely, whatever things are of good report, if there is any virtue and if there is anything praiseworthy—meditate on these things.

Psalms 138:7

Though I walk in the midst of trouble, You will revive me;

You will stretch out Your hand
Against the wrath of my enemies,
And Your right hand will save me.

John 14:27
Peace I leave with you, My peace I give to you; not as the world
gives do I give to you. Let not your heart be troubled, neither let it
be afraid.

II Corinthians 4:8-9
We are hard-pressed on every side, yet not crushed; we are
perplexed, but not in despair; ⁹ persecuted, but not forsaken;
struck down, but not destroyed—

Isaiah 51:11
So the ransomed of the Lord shall return, and come to Zion with
singing, with everlasting joy on their heads. They shall obtain joy
and gladness; Sorrow and sighing shall flee away.

Philippians 1:6
Being confident of this very thing, that He who has begun a good
work in you will perform it until the day of Jesus Christ;

Psalm 31:24
Be of good courage,
And He shall strengthen your heart,
All you who hope in the Lord.

Hebrews 10:35-36
³⁵ Therefore do not cast away your confidence, which has great
reward. ³⁶ For you have need of endurance, so that after you have
done the will of God, you may receive the promise:

Galatians 6:9
And let us not grow weary while doing good, for in due season
we shall reap if we do not lose heart.

Psalm 34:17
The righteous cry out, and the Lord hears, And delivers them out of all their troubles.

Psalm 46:1
God is our refuge and strength,
A very present help in trouble.

Spritual Warfare Prayer

Deliverance makes the rough places smooth and the crooked places straight. Your words and prayers have tremendous power to destroy the works of darkness. You have the power to bind and loose according to Matthew 18:1. Bind means to confuse, restrict arrest, apprehend, take charge of, put a stop to, and lock up. We have legal authority in the name of Jesus to bind the works of Satan. Loose means to unchain, unlock, disconnect, break away, detach, and get free. We must be loosed from curses such as evil inheritance, familiar spirits, etc. You have the legal authority in the name of Jesus to loose yourself and others whom we minister from these destroying influences.

Those who experience deliverance and release will see notable changes. Sometimes the change is instantaneous and other times it is progressive, but patience is necessary to see your breakthrough. In Deuteronomy 7:22, God promised Israel that he would drive the enemy out little by little. You must understand this principle or you will become weary in your praying. You cannot become discouraged in your own deliverance.

Deliverance is the children's bread. You will see multiplied miracles through warfare prayer such as supernatural healing, hidden things exposed, and stubborn obstacles such as poverty, divination, torment and confusion will be removed. You will put a stop to those things in your life and in the lives of those we minister to.

♦Heavenly Father, I thank you that no weapon formed against us shall prosper.

♦I thank you that every tongue and every word that rises against me in judgment, you condemn.

♦I thank you Heavenly Father that this is the heritage of the servants of the Lord and our righteousness is from you according to Isaiah 54:17.

Heavenly Father, in the name of Jesus Christ, I pull down every demonic stronghold of _____ and cast aside in dry places and they never return again in the name of Jesus.

II Corinthians 10:2-4, "But I beg you that when I am present I may not be bold with that confidence by which I intend to be bold against some, who think of us as if we walked according to the flesh. ³ For though we walk in the flesh, we do not war according to the flesh. ⁴ For the weapons of our warfare are not carnal but mighty in God for pulling down strongholds,".

♦Father, I thank you that the yoke will be destroyed because of the anointing oil. Isaiah 10:27.

♦Heavenly Father, I ask you to break and destroy any yokes of bondage including things such as fear, lust, drug abuse, sexual impurity, along with all of their works, roots, fruits, tentacles, and links that are in my life in the name of Jesus. I ask that you render them powerless and harmless. Nullify, destroy, and cancel the power of any evil spirit, demonic spirit, strongman, and messenger of Satan in the name of Jesus.

♦I apply the blood of Jesus over witchcraft prayers that try to come into my presence, marriage, and telephone lines in the name of Jesus Christ of Nazareth.

♦In accordance with John 16:23, Heavenly Father, I ask you to give me deliverance and freedom from all these bondages in the name of Jesus Christ.

♦I am delivered from the power of darkness and translated in God's kingdom in the name of Jesus (Colossians 1:13). I bind of the tormenting spirit in the name of Jesus. I loose God's Holy presence.

♦I am Christ's friend, chosen and appointed, by God's Holy Spirit to bear His fruit (John 15:15-16).

♦Heavenly Father, in the name of Jesus, I destroy any psychic, witchcraft, or ungodly, soulish prayers that have been prayed, spoken over me, my children, my church in order to control or manipulate me. Be scattered now, the blood of Jesus is against you.

Ephesians 6:12, "For we do not wrestle against flesh and blood, but against principalities, against powers, against the rulers of the darkness of this age, against spiritual hosts of wickedness in the heavenly places."

HOSPITAL PRAYER

♦Heavenly Father I ask you to loose your angels in great abundant into _____

(name)

presence, the presence of every doctor, every nurse, in his/her room, the surgery unit, and recovery.

♦Now I bind all sickness of Satanic evil, wicked demons, lying, and tormenting spirits of strongman, along with all their works, tentacles, fruits, roots, and links, and spirits in the name of Jesus.

♦I decree Psalm 91, the Lord is a deliverer. I ask, in the name of Jesus, that every organ, every gland, every cell, every muscle, every ligament in her/his body be made whole, totally free, total liberated, and totally saved from all evil, wicked demons. The blood of Jesus prevails over this body.

♦I declare these sicknesses to die from the root from viruses, fungi, infections, bacteria, MRSA, inflammations, radical cells, abnormal growths, cancers, tumors, and disorders of any kind in every cell in his/her body.

♦According to your word in Matthew 16:19, I have the keys to the kingdom of Heaven. I loose strongman from this house (body). Demonic spirits, diseases, unclean spirits, foul spirits, and witchcraft spirits, we take this (house) body back. This is the temple of God in the name of Jesus.

♦Heavenly Father, I plead the blood of Jesus Christ over this (brother, sister, friend) from the top of his/her head to the soles of his/her feet. All sicknesses and diseases are ashes under my feet.

•Heavenly Father, I ask you now according to your word John 16:23 to release your miracle virtue, your miracles anointed into this room in the name of Jesus Christ of Nazareth.

•I command anointed miracles to flow through every part of his/her body.

•Heavenly Father, I ask you to let the Holy Spirit of God manifest every miracle and every healing that you have given this (man, woman, child) in Jesus name.

•Heavenly Father, I ask you in the name of Jesus to give divine healing and divine health, wholeness, and newness of life according to your word; Thank you Father in the name of your son Jesus.

•Heavenly Father, I loose extra angels around the hospital, the nurses, the doctors, and other patients. Leave them there as long as _____ is in the hospital, to guard and protect him/her.

•Heavenly Father, I ask you to render harmless, nullify, cancel, and destroy the power of any evil demonic stronghold or messenger of Satan that tries to enter into the presence of _____ in this hospital in Jesus' name. Amen

THIS YEAR TAKE AUTHORITY

Jesus described the Word as seed. "Now the parable is this: The seed is the word of God". God's Word of Promise will never be barren. The power in His word will always fulfill the promise of His word. We must understand time, timing, and God given missions to triumph. The Lord designed time with a built in blessing for us to claim and walk in to.

Psalm 65:11, "You crown the year with your goodness, And Your paths drip with abundance."

Ecclesiastes 7:8, "The end of a thing is better than its beginning; the patient in spirit is better than the proud in spirit."

Job 8:7, "Though thy beginning was small, yet thy latter end should greatly increase."

Know that the end of this year will be better than how you began it. You will end this year a better person. You will become better spiritually, physically, emotionally, and financially. There is an increase of goodness for you just expect it, believe it, and receive it. Trust and believe God.

Psalm 102:13, "Thou shall arise, and have mercy upon Zion for the time to favor her, yea, the set time is come."

If God can get it through to you, God will give it to you

Confession:

♦I will not expire this year. I shall be revived for honor and fruitfulness in Jesus name.

♦I proclaim and declare my season of unceasing favor to manifest the glory of God in Jesus name.

♦My blessing for this year will not die therefore, arise and locate me by fire in the name of Jesus.

♦Every power attempting to stop my breakthrough in order to frustrate me, go now in Jesus name.

♦Every power of distraction assigned against my life this year, fall down and die in the name of Jesus.

♦I take authority over this year, in the name of Jesus.

•I decree that all of the elements will cooperate with me this year.

•I decree that the elemental forces refuses and will not cooperate with my enemies.

•I pull down all negative energies planning to operate against my life this year.

•This is the year the Lord has made, I will rejoice and be glad in it.

•I dismantle any power uttering incantations to capture this year. I render such incantations and satanic prayer null and void.

•I retrieve this year out of their hands, in the name of Jesus.

•Spirits of favor, counsel, might and power, come upon me, in the name of Jesus.

•I shall excel this year and nothing shall defile me.

•I shall possess the gates of my enemies.

•The Lord shall anoint me with the oil of gladness above my fellows.

•The fire of the enemy shall not burn me.

•My ears shall hear good news and I shall not hear the voice of the enemy.

•My future is secured in Christ, in the name of Jesus.

•God has created me to do some definite services.

•He has committed into my hands some assignments which He has not committed to anyone.

•He has not created me for nothing. I shall do well. I shall do His work. I shall be an agent of peace.

•I will trust Him in whatever I do and wherever I am.

♦I can never be thrown away or downgraded. There will be no poverty in my body, in my soul, in my spirit, or in my life this year.

♦The anointing of God upon my life gives me favor in the eyes of God and man all the days of my life.

♦I shall not labor in vain. I shall walk this year in victory and liberty of the spirit.

♦This year, the Lord will make me a winner and a candidate of uncommon testimonies, in the name of Jesus.

♦This year, I receive daily bread, good seed to sow every time, and money to spend always, in the name of Jesus.

♦In this year, my life will advertise the glory of God, in Jesus' name.

♦I cancel all appointments with sorrow, tragedy, and evil cries this year, in the name of Jesus.

♦This year, I will encounter and experience a full scale laughter in the name of Jesus.

♦From now on, blood-thirsty demons and robbers will flee at my presence, in the name of Jesus.

♦Whether I am on the sea, in the air, or on the road, the evil forces there will bow to my authority, in the name of Jesus.

♦Anything I have waited for a long time shall be miraculously delivered to me this year, in the name of Jesus.

♦My Father, make me and my family members completely immune to any form of sickness or disease this year, in the name of Jesus.

♦This year, I put myself and members of my family into the protective envelope of divine fire, in the name of Jesus.

•This year, I will do the will of God and I will serve God, in the name of Jesus.

•This year, I will have unconquerable victory, in Jesus' name.

•This year, like clay in the hands of the potter, the Lord will make what He wants out of my life, in the name of Jesus.

•This year, the Lord will do with me whatever He wants, in the name of Jesus.

•This year, the Lord will make me the head and not tail, in Jesus' name.

•This year, every snare of the fowler assigned against me shall perish, in Jesus' name.

•This year, I render the habitation of darkness assigned against me desolate, in the name of Jesus.

•This year, divine deposits shall settle in my life, in the name of Jesus.

•This year, I enter into the covenant of favor, in the name of Jesus.

•This year, the anointing of success and fruitfulness shall rest on me, in the name of Jesus.

•This year, I will not be a candidate of sweating without result, in Jesus' name.

•This year, all obstacles in my way of progress shall be dismantled, in the name of Jesus.

•This year, my God shall arise and my stubborn pursuers shall scatter, in Jesus' name.

•This year, those that mock me in the past shall celebrate with me, in Jesus' name.

•This year, my Goliath and Hamman shall experience destruction, in the name of Jesus.

•This year, every power assigned to cut my life short shall die, in the name of Jesus.

•This year, my prayers shall always provoke angelic violence for my good, in Jesus' name.

•This year, I shall speak and my words shall bring testimonies, in the name of Jesus.

•Thou that trouble the _____ the God of Elijah shall trouble you today.

•Every enemy of _____ scatter, in the name of Jesus.

•God, arise and uproot anything you did not plant inside _____ in the name of Jesus

•Let the fire of revival fall on _____ in the name of Jesus.

•I am delivered by the blood of Jesus.

THREE DAY CONFESSION

In Genesis 27:40, Jacob stole Esau's birthright. He then he stole his blessings. When Esau cried out to his father, Isaac, by the spirit of God Isaac said, "When thou shalt have dominion, thou shalt break his yoke from off thy neck". This simply means that when you get tired of Satan's attack that is the day of your freedom.

Shout!!!! Lord, I am tired. I want my freedom and my blessings!

You may have opened some doors to the enemy to keep attacking you through anger, food, adultery, and debt. But the moment the fire of God stirs up the Holy Ghost in you over your situation, you will pray with spiritual violence and every power or yoke will be broken.

Shout!!!! Devil you steal no more of my birthrights!

♦Let the seven fold stand and be raised on all of my enemies in the name of Jesus.

♦In the name of Jesus, I nullify every satanic embarrassment.

♦O Lord, make me a channel of blessing.

♦Every evil stronghold, be bound in the name of Jesus.

♦I cut down familiar spirits with a two edged sword with the word of God.

♦Let the angels of war be released on my behalf in Jesus name.

♦I remove myself from every demonic, satanic bus stop or train stop in the name of Jesus.

♦Let every evil thing done against me, family, church between the hour 12:01 p.m. and 6:00 a.m., catch on fire and burn up in Jesus name.

♦I command my name to be removed from the book of backward steps in the name of Jesus name.

♦I bind all anti-miracle demons in every area of my life in Jesus name.

♦I destroy all the webs of Satan against my life, my family, and my church in name of Jesus.

♦Every spiritual equipment set against me are broken and shattered in pieces in the name of Jesus.

•I break all the curses issued against my future and progress in the name of Jesus.

•Let agents of demonic delay begin to loose their hold over my life.

•Let agents of poverty, debt, and frustration begin to loose their hold over my life, church, and family in the name of Jesus.

•I cancel every careless word which I have spoken and which Satan is using against me in the name of Jesus.

•My whole life is invisible to demonic observance in the name of Jesus.

•I remove my name from the book of tragedy.

•Let the enemy fall into the pit dug for my sake in Jesus' name.

•All curses issued by my spouse are nullified in the name of Jesus.

•Lord, reschedule my enemies to a useless assignment.

•I refuse to be spiritually amputated in the name of Jesus.

•Lord, let all physical and spiritual sicknesses flee now in the name of Jesus.

•Heavenly Father let all my locked up blessings come out of the prison in the name of Jesus.

•O Lord, give me a miracle that would dumbfound this city in the name of Jesus.

•Lord let my name become fire, thunder, in the mouths or hands of those calling it for evil purposes in the name of Jesus.

•I bind every evil activity now and I speak to my atmosphere; Change now in the name of Jesus.

I Am Sentenced To Victory

•I loose your hold upon my life, Satan, in the name of Jesus.

•Satan, I command you to be separated from me now.

•I dismantle every satanic dust bin fashioned against me, in the name of Jesus.

•I dismantle every evil throne that has been installed against me. I plead the blood of Jesus.

•I overthrow every demonic, satanic, judgment, directed against me.

•I close down every satanic broadcasting station fashioned against my name, in the name of Jesus.

•I cast the spirit behind my problem into the pit and send it back to the sender.

•I dismantle every demonic opposition to my breakthroughs, in Jesus name.

•Every satanic case filed against my life is closed by the blood of Jesus.

•Divine favor is in every blessing of my life, in the name of Jesus.

•Blood of Jesus, disconnect my life from failure at the edge of breakthrough, in the name of Jesus.

•Let the foundation of my life be prepared to carry divine prosperity, in the name of Jesus.

•Holy Spirit of fire, destroy every garment of reproach in my life, Hallelujah, in the name of Jesus.

•Every evil guest, do not locate my address, in the name of Jesus.

•Every Evil River mocking my effects, dry up now, in the name of Jesus.

•I refuse to pick the wrong materials from the bank of life, in the name of Jesus.

•I destroy all secret power sources fashioned against me, in the name of Jesus.

•I refuse to lose any ground in my life to the enemy.

•Let the blood of Jesus erase all handwritings of poverty in my life in the name of Jesus.

•Just as the grave cannot hold Jesus, no grave will hold my miracles, in the name of Jesus.

•I withdraw the authority belonging to any demonic object fashioned against me.

•Every evil grip upon my spirit, loose your hold now, in the name of Jesus.

•I receive the anointing to disgrace satanic arrows, in the name of Jesus.

•Let the military angels of the Almighty pursue and attack my attackers, in the name of Jesus.

•I break every evil padlock put upon my church, family, business, and home, be cast down and ousted never to return, in the name of Jesus.

•Let every satanic law programmed into me be terminated, in the name of Jesus.

•Resistances to my breakthroughs crumble, in the name of Jesus.

•Let every dead organ (amputated blessing, dead marriage, paralyzed potential, battered emotion, lifeless business) receive the resurrection power of the Lord Jesus Christ now.

Pray until you know it is done

A PRAYER FOR THE NATION

II Chronicles 7:14

"If My people who are called by My name will humble themselves, and pray and seek My face, and turn from their wicked ways, then I will hear from heaven, and will forgive their sin and heal their land."

•Heavenly Father, as a prayer warrior, I humble myself and pray on behalf of this nation for the healing of our land.

•Father, I seek your face and pray that you would deliver us from the problems of crime, violence, drugs, and lawlessness.

•I pray that you would heal us of our economic problems.

•Father, I pray that you would restore the fear of the Lord back upon this nation in the name of Jesus.

•Heavenly Father, forgive us for abandoning you as our first love. Father, I pray that you would have mercy upon us in the name of the Father, Son, and the Holy Ghost, according to your loving kindness.

•Heavenly Father, I decree restoration of love back into our nations, regions, cities, and states in the name of Jesus.

♦Father, I pray that by your grace and mercy, you would deliver us and spare us from catastrophic disasters such as earthquakes, hurricanes, tornadoes, and other natural catastrophes.

♦I pray that you would give our leaders, (mayors, police, governor, senators, employers, pastors, President of the United States and his cabinet), Godly inspired counsel, decisions, and directions for this nation.

♦By the authority of the name of Jesus Christ, I come against every demonic spirit, every principality, and every spirit of wickedness in high places over or against this nation. I plead the blood of Jesus. I command these spirits to scatter now.

♦I bind their demonic power and influence on our nation. I bind every hindering spirit that would attempt to bring down our nation spiritually, socially, or economically in the name of Jesus.

♦I loose the fear of God into our nation in the name of Jesus.

♦I decree that every satanic and demonic weapon that is formed against this nation to be helpless, powerless, inoperable, and ineffective by the power and the authority of the name of Jesus.

Psalm 91:3-15 states [3] Surely He shall deliver you from the snare of the fowler
And from the perilous pestilence.
[4] He shall cover you with His feathers,
And under His wings you shall take refuge;
His truth shall be your shield and buckler.
[5] You shall not be afraid of the terror by night,
Nor of the arrow that flies by day,
[6] Nor of the pestilence that walks in darkness,
Nor of the destruction that lays waste at noonday.
[7] A thousand may fall at your side,
And ten thousand at your right hand;
But it shall not come near you.

⁸ Only with your eyes shall you look,
And see the reward of the wicked.
⁹ Because you have made the Lord, who is my refuge,
Even the Most High, your dwelling place,
¹⁰ No evil shall befall you,
Nor shall any plague come near your dwelling;
¹¹ For He shall give His angels charge over you,
To keep you in all your ways.
¹² In their hands they shall bear you up,
Lest you dash your foot against a stone.
¹³ You shall tread upon the lion and the cobra,
The young lion and the serpent you shall trample underfoot.
¹⁴ "Because he has set his love upon Me, therefore I will deliver him;
I will set him on high, because he has known My name.
¹⁵ He shall call upon Me, and I will answer him;
I will be with him in trouble;
I will deliver him and honor him."

♦Let our leaders be just, and let him rule by the fear of the Lord. Let all the idolaters in this nation be confounded in the name of Jesus. I pray for the healing water to flow into my nation Ezekiel 47:9. Let the poor and needy people of this nation be delivered.

♦Let this nation be filled with the knowledge of the glory of the Lord in Jesus name. Let my nation look to the Lord and be saved (Isaiah 45:22).

♦I pray that the parched places in my nation will become a pool and every thirsty part springs water.

♦I pray that my nation will submit to the rule and reign of Jesus Christ. Let your glory be declared among my people, and your wonders in this nation (Psalm 96:20).

◆Father, In the name of Jesus, I pray for your divine will to be done in and throughout this nation, as well as through the lives of the people who dwell in it. In Jesus name I pray, AMEN

MARRIAGE

I declare my marriage to be whole and sound in the name of Jesus

Proverbs 18:22
"He who finds a wife finds a good thing, And obtains favor from the Lord.

Genesis 2:18
"And the Lord God said, "It is not good that man should be alone; I will make him a helper comparable to him."

Genesis 2:24
"Therefore a man shall leave his father and mother and be joined to his wife, and they shall become one flesh."

Hosea 2:19
"I will betroth you to Me forever;
Yes, I will betroth you to Me
In righteousness and justice,
In loving kindness and mercy".

◆Heavenly Father, I come boldly to the throne of grace for your help in restoring my marriage in the name of Jesus.

◆Lord, I come humbly before you asking that you heal what is broken in this marriage.

•I take my place, standing in the gap, for my husband/wife against the Devil and his demons until the salvation of God is manifested in his/her life.

•Heavenly Father, I am looking for your plan and your answer for my life. It is my desire to be married and stay with my spouse until death.

•Father I ask that we be delivered from the spirit of rejection and accepted in the beloved name of Jesus.

•I bind the spirit of divorce and separation. Satan, I loose you from your assignment in Jesus' name.

•Therefore, Lord I ask you to speak to my heart and heal my hurts so we may be reconciled to making this marriage work in Jesus' name.

•I ask you Lord to help us, that we will walk in the love, esteeming and delighting in one another as Christ loved us and gave himself up for us.

•I plead the Blood of Jesus over this marriage. I have come to my senses and escaped out of the snare of the Devil that had me captive.

•My marriage has been restored by the grace of God. I stand firm and confident knowing that Satan has no power over this marriage.

•Help me Lord to remain sane and sober-minded, temperate and disciplined, because I love my spouse and my children. Whom the Son has set free is free indeed.

RELEASE CHILDREN FROM BONDAGE

God has a plan for children. He wants to use them to defeat the enemy. But the young people find it difficult to distinguish between the true and the counterfeit, they are constantly receiving information. One touch from Jesus was enough to open blind eyes, heal long standing infirmities, and set the captives free. No matter the strength or the duration of the bondage, just one touch was enough.

Psalm 127

♦I break all covenant bondage in the name of Jesus.

♦I paralyze evil reinforcement and dissolve satanic network.

♦I decree that neither sickness nor plague will come upon my child in the name of Jesus.

♦Father, I decree soundness, good health, and wholeness to their spirit, their soul, and their body in Jesus' name.

♦O Lord, I decree that my child will be saved at an early age.

♦I apply the blood of Jesus to every stubborn problem in my child's life.

♦Heavenly Father, my child will be strong in the Lord and in the power of His might.

♦Heavenly Father, I thank you for the benefits and provisions, in blood of Jesus, for my son/daughter.

Deliverance for your children

Infants and young children need to be prayed for against unfriendly friends and demonic initiation against through food and things. They need to be constantly placed under the protection of the blood of Jesus.

•My child will have wisdom and knowledge and stature in favor with Holy God and man. Luke 2:53

Psalm 8:2
Out of the mouth of babes and nursing infants, you have ordained strength, Because of Your enemies, that you may silence the enemy and the avenger.

1 John 4:4
You are of God, little children, and have overcome them, because He who is in you is greater than he who is in the world.

Isaiah 8:10
Take counsel together, but it will come to nothing speak the word, but it will not stand, For God is with us.

•My children will not become a misdirected arrow.

•I release my child(ren) from the bondage of evil domination

•Every evil influence and activity toward my child(ren) be nullified in the name of Jesus

•I bind every blinding spirit of their mind and I loose the sight of the Lord in them.

•I call every curse and evil covenant passed down to my son/daughter be cancelled now in the name of Jesus

•I command wholeness, soundness, and perfection into my child's heart, eyes, ears, skin, bones, and teeth in Jesus name

•I dismantle every demonic kingdom built in the street for destruction and death. I break the threefold cord of death, hell, and the grave in the name of Jesus

*If your child(ren) are going through demonic, satanic situations…reverse it and send it back to the sender.

•I command everything that will prevent my son/daughter from being a blessing be totally shattered in the name of Jesus.

•I bind every negative ancestral spirit and command it to loose its hold upon my son/daughter in the name of Jesus.

•I command any power that wants to convert my son/daughter into a nuisance; I call it to be paralyzed in the name of Jesus.

•I silence every evil bearing dog barking against my /daughter in the name of Jesus.

•The written word said, I am in Jesus whom thou persecute; it is hard for these to kick against the pricks. Acts 9:5

•My son/daughter will begin to have difficulty finding his/her path of wickedness.

SPIRIT OF DIVINATION

ACTS 16:16-18 "Now it happened, as we went to prayer, that a certain slave girl possessed with a spirit of divination met us, who brought her masters much profit by fortune-telling. This girl followed Paul and us, and cried out, saying, "These men are the servants of the Most High God, who proclaim to us the way of salvation." And this she did for many days.
But Paul, greatly annoyed, turned and said to the spirit, "I command you in the name of Jesus Christ to come out of her." And he came out that very hour."

•Strongmen call Spirit of Divination; I bind you in the name of Jesus along with all of your works, roots, fruits, tentacles, and links that are in my life, family, and church.

♦I command and bind rebellion, levitation, dungeons and dragons, magic, tarot cards, crystal balls, warlocks, enchanters, witches, pride, arrogance, ego, horoscopes, zodiac, fortune telling, and sooth sayers, catch on fire, die from the roots. I loose you from us and I force you into outer darkness in the name of Jesus Christ.

♦I bind you in the name of Jesus Christ and declare that all of your works, roots, fruits, tentacles, links, and spirits are dead works in my life and church.

♦I loose into me today the Holy Spirit and His gifts according to 1 Corinthians 2:9-12 "Hallelujah"

SPIRIT OF ERROR

We are of God. He who knows God hears us; he who is not of God does not hear us. By this we know the spirit of truth and the spirit of error.

♦I bind you in the name of Jesus and declare that all of your works, roots, tentacles, links, and spirits are dead, disconnected, and discontinued in our lives in Jesus name
♦Mental confusion, fear
♦Pain, depression
♦Foolish talking
♦Hindrances to bible study
♦Dullness of comprehension listening to sermon/moving gifts of Holy Spirit
♦Unteachable

Proverbs 10:17

He who keeps instruction is in the way of life, But he who refuses correction goes astray.

Proverbs 12:1-2
Whoever loves instruction loves knowledge, But he who hates correction is stupid.[2] A good man obtains favor from the Lord, But a man of wicked intentions He will condemn.

2 Timothy 4:1-4
I charge you therefore before God and the Lord Jesus Christ, who will judge the living and the dead at[a] His appearing and His kingdom: Preach the word! Be ready in season and out of season. Convince, rebuke, exhort, with all longsuffering and teaching. For the time will come when they will not endure sound doctrine, but according to their own desires, because they have itching ears, they will heap up for themselves teachers; and they will turn their ears away from the truth, and be turned aside to fables.

◆Error

Proverbs 14:33
Wisdom rests in the heart of him who has understanding, But what is in the heart of fools is made known.

2 Peter 3:16-17
as also in all his epistles, speaking in them of these things, in which are some things hard to understand, which untaught and unstable people twist to their own destruction, as they do also the rest of the Scriptures. You therefore, beloved, since you know this beforehand, beware lest you also fall from your own steadfastness, being led away with the error of the wicked;

◆Resistance to biblical and spiritual truth

◆I bind the strongmen spirit of error and loose you from me and my church. I command you not to come back into our presence again. Cut the umbilical cord of error.

THIS WEEK PRAYER

♦Every man and woman assigned to bless and help me this week, this week, this year arise where ever you are and locate me in the name of Jesus.

♦I decree every evil programmed into this week (against my church, my life, my family, etc), scatter now, never be connected again in the name of Jesus.

♦Where ever you are appear, locate me in this week now in Jesus.

♦Wherever you are _____appear and locate me in this week, now, in Jesus name.

♦I declare that my flesh will listen to God's voice this week. Devil catch on fire and die, for the blood of Jesus is against you (say seven times, lay hands on yourself).

♦Every demonic, satanic spirit assigned to flesh this week, I cast down. I am not your candidate; therefore die in the name of Jesus.

♦I separate me from any failure in this week in the name of Jesus

♦The doors of opportunity shall be opened to me this week in the name of Jesus

♦O Lord, my Father, appear to me in my situation as a very present help this week in the name of Jesus

♦Every demonic war of attrition waged to wear me down and out, hear the Word of the Lord and cease now and never return in the mighty name of Jesus

♦God is in the middle of all my trouble and he shall not be moved. God shall help just at the break of dawn. (Shout this week---- victory)

I Give God praise and glory, thank God for answers in this week's prayers. This prayer will carry you through your lifetime.

TWILIGHT PRAYER

♦Every midnight (twilight) evil power, I cast you down now in the name of Jesus.

♦I pull down every strong hold power that is used at night to steal from me and my family, die in the name of Jesus.

♦Every warfare occurring at night that has prospered against me to die now, and the blood of Jesus is against you.

♦Powers of the night assigned to disgrace me; I send it back to the sender in the name of Jesus.

♦Every satanic activity against me in the night; be buried alive in the name of Jesus.

♦Powers of the night troubling my dream life scatter in the name of Jesus.

♦Wicked marks that have been put on my life at night be wiped off by the blood of Jesus, in the name of Jesus.

♦Every power blocking the way of my complete joy scatters now in the name of Jesus.

♦Every satanic power that does not want to let my family and me go be confused, in the name of Jesus.

◆Powers of the night troubling my habitation die in the name of Jesus.

◆Every power searching for my face in demonic mirrors, your time is up! Burn up in the name of Jesus.

◆Wickedness of the night assigned against my life, expire in the name of Jesus.

◆Tonight, Heavenly Father, provoke your violent angels to fight for me, in the name of Jesus.

◆Tonight, every witchcraft bird flying against me and my church have no agreement in their assignment, die in the name of Jesus.

◆Every enemy that came while I was sleeping, your time is up! I cast you down to dry places, in the name of Jesus.

◆Pharaoh of my father's house sinks in the red sea, in the name of Jesus.

◆I shut down the Anti-prosperity chains on my hands; I'm not your candidate, in the name of Jesus.

You can provoke God with fearful praises and pray at midnight like Paul and Silas. It is a time of release from every spiritual prison, when you utilize the mystery of midnight prayers, it would initiate the earthquake of deliverance that would set you free. At twilight, David recovered all (1 Samuel 30:17).

Acts 16:25
But at midnight Paul and Silas were praying and singing hymns to God, and the prisoners were listening to them.

Job 4:20, "They are destroyed from morning to evening: they perish forever without any regarding it." The stronghold of the mighty can be destroyed at midnight.

The twilight talks of darkness are the absence of light and presence of blindness. It is for rest and unsuitable for labor. It is favorable to the purposes of wickedness. Wild beasts seek their prey at night. Shepherds watch over their sheep at night. The twilight is a period of severe calamities. Darkness has binding powers, it limits activities. It has separating powers. That is when all that is evil and unworthy of light is let loose.

Psalm 119:62, "At midnight I will rise to give thanks unto thee because of thy righteous judgments."

Exodus 11:4, "And Moses said, Thus saith the LORD, About midnight will I go out into the midst of Egypt:"

Exodus 12:29, "And it came to pass, that at midnight the LORD smote all the firstborn in the land of Egypt, from the firstborn of Pharaoh that sat on his throne unto the firstborn of the captive that was in the dungeon; and all the firstborn of cattle." You can utilize the midnight hour to break the back bone of the enemy.

Judges 16:3, "And Samson lay till midnight, and arose at midnight, and took the doors of the gate of the city, and the two posts, and went away with them, bar and all, and put them upon his shoulders, and carried them up to the top of an hill that is before Hebron." You can follow the example of Samson to uproot the gate of the enemy at midnight.

Ruth 3:8, "And it came to pass at midnight, that the man was afraid, and turned himself: and, behold, a woman lay at his feet.

If you want to speedily find your godly spouse, either wife or husband you can follow the example of Ruth by praying at midnight.

Matthew 25:6, "And at midnight there was a cry made, Behold, the bridegroom cometh; go ye out to meet him."

Luke 11:5, "And he said unto them, Which of you shall have a friend, and shall go unto him at midnight, and say unto him, Friend, lend me three loaves;

Midnight hour is the time to Ask, Seek and Knock the doors. Your petition at this hour makes things begin to happen for you. That hour is a weak period for the children of the bond woman.

1 Kings 3:20, "And she arose at midnight, and took my son from beside me, while thine handmaid slept, and laid it in her bosom, and laid her dead child in my bosom The midnight hour is the best time to catch the thief that came to steal, kill and destroy, while men slept.

2 Kings 6:13-14, "And he said, Go and spy where he is, that I may send and fetch him. And it was told him, saying, Behold, he is in Dothan. Therefore sent he thither horses, and chariots, and a great host: and they came by night, and compassed the city about." The midnight hours are their working hours.

DECLARATION/AFFIRMATION I AM IN CHRIST

◆I am alive with Christ. Galatians 2:20

◆I am established to the end. Romans 1:11

◆I am strong in the Lord. Ephesians 6:10

◆I am sealed with the Holy Spirit of Promise. Ephesians 1:13

◆I am a new creature in Christ. Corinthians 5:17

◆I am forgiven of all of my sins and washed in the blood. 1 John 1:9, Ephesians 1:7, Hebrews 9:14, Colossians 1:14

◆I am free from condemnation. John 5:24

◆I am purposely built and uniquely designed for success.

•I am being changed into His image. 1 Corinthians 3:18

•I am firmly rooted, built up, and established in the faith. Colossians 2:7

•I am righteous and holy.

•I am enslaved to God.

•I am light of the world and salt of the earth. Matthew 5:13-14

•I am God's workmanship created in Christ Jesus for good work. Ephesians 2:20

•I am dead with Christ and dead to the power of sin's rule over my life. Romans 6:1-6

•I am the apple of my Father's eye. Deuteronomy 32:10

•I am transformed by the renewing of my mind.

•I am blessed spiritually, financially, and emotionally.

•I am completed in Him. Colossians 2:10

•I am redeemed from the curse of the law of sin and death. Galatians 3:13

•I am one of God's living stones and I am being brought up as a spiritual house.

•I am reconciled to God and I am a minister of reconciliation. 2 Corinthians 5:18-19.

•I am an heir of Christ I'm no longer a slave I am a daughter/son of the living God. Galatians 4:6-7.

•I am protected by God's angels. Psalms 91:14-16.

•I am healed by His stripes, your word say that my healing shall spring forth speedily. Isaiah 53:5, Isaiah 58:8

•I declare that I am overtaken with blessing. Deuteronomy 28:2

•I am bought with a price, I am not my own, I belong to God. 1 Corinthians 6:19-20

•I press toward the mark of the prize the high calling of God.

PROPHESY

•I prophesy, Earth to get in her place to receive Heavenly instruction on my behalf in the name of Jesus.

•I prophesy life to the failing in Jesus name.

•I prophesy to everything that is dull and unfinished and command it to shine and be complete in the name of Jesus.

•I prophesy to the Spirit of Gaza; Leave my territory. Things that keep me in battle, go NOW in the name of Jesus. I apply the blood of Jesus over my ground.

•I call the rebuke of the Lord upon the devourers set against me.

•I take authority over the territory that the Lord has given me. I prophesy to her womb to produce, multiply to me now in the name of Jesus.

•I prophesy to that which is held up (my healing and hidden finances), or down and oppressed. I declare it shall rise now.

•I declare spiritual, physical, mental, emotional, and material nourishment to be placed back into my life in the name of Jesus.

•I command the spirit of slack to tighten up now so that standard of the Almighty God may reign.

•I command that which will cause me to not hear, understand God's will and voice: leave my presence now.

◆I prophesy that my seed shall live and fulfill the perfect will of God on the Earth.

◆I prophesy the blessing shall flow through my (their) lineage and all curses are blocked and bound in the name of Jesus.

◆Heavenly Father, I declare and decree new territory and new locations, this year, in the name of Jesus.

◆Heavenly Father, you give me authority to tread down the wicked until they become ashes under my feet.

◆In Jesus name, I prophesy to the trim and command it to be fat. Hallelujah!!!

◆I prophesy life with my tongue and bind death, in the name of Jesus. (**Shout Loud three times**)

◆I prophesy to those closed doors, open now, in the name of Jesus.

◆I prophesy to the wind of morning, our church will and shall stand; Great manifold blessings physically, spiritually, and financially in the name of Jesus. The blood of Jesus covers our territory and **we take it all back!!!**

◆I prophesy a mass physical growth at _____.

◆Heavenly Father, I prophesy mass revival in the North eastern region now in Jesus' name.

◆Today, great visitation of God's spirit will reveal uncommon favor and doors that the Lord ordains are wide open to the saints. I plead the blood of Jesus over it now.

◆I prophesy that every vicious cycle over my territory die now, I call a whirlwind to break it into pieces and never connect again in the name of Jesus.

Strength

Yeshua-You are my savior, love, Lord Shalom -peace, strength, deliverer, righteousness, companion, sufficiency, fulfillment, and everything.

Daniel 10:19
And he said, "O man greatly beloved, fear not! Peace be to you; be strong, yes, be strong!" So when he spoke to me I was strengthened, and said, "Let my lord speak, for you have strengthened me."

Psalms 119:28
My soul melts from heaviness;
Strengthen me according to Your word.

Ephesians 3:16-17
[16] that He would grant you, according to the riches of His glory, to be strengthened with might through His Spirit in the inner man, [17] that Christ may dwell in your hearts through faith; that you, being rooted and grounded in love,

Colossians 1:10-12
that you may walk worthy of the Lord, fully pleasing Him, being fruitful in every good work and increasing in the knowledge of God; 11 strengthened with all might, according to His glorious power, for all patience and longsuffering with joy; 12 giving thanks to the Father who has qualified us to be partakers of the inheritance of the saints in the light

Nehemiah 8:10
Then he said to them, "Go your way, eat the fat, drink the sweet, and send portions to those for whom nothing is prepared; for this day is holy to our Lord. Do not sorrow, for the joy of the Lord is your strength."

Isaiah 41:10
Fear not, for I am with you;
Be not dismayed, for I am your God.
I will strengthen you, Yes, I will help you, I will uphold you with
My righteous right hand.

Proverbs 8:14
Counsel is mine, and sound wisdom;
I am understanding, I have strength.

Ephesians 6:10, 13
[10]Finally, my brethren, be strong in the Lord and in the power
of His might. [13]Therefore take up the whole armor of God, that
you may be able to withstand in the evil day, and having done
all, to stand.

ATTACKING THE ENEMY
OF YOUR CALLING

Isaiah 59:19
"So shall they fear
The name of the Lord from the west,
And His glory from the rising of the sun;
When the enemy comes in like a flood,
The Spirit of the Lord will lift up a standard against him"

Specifically Designed For Ministers

Things are not moving in your ministry. Your ministerial
life is being attacked by disappointment and division. Signs and

wonders completely elude your ministry. You are unable to focus your attention on what God expects you to do. You want to sharpen you spiritual sword. I pray the Lord will fortify our inner man with fire so that we can attack the enemies of our calling.

Confession

Matthew 16:18 says "And I also say to you that you are Peter, and on this rock I will build my church, and the gates of Hades shall not prevail against it."

♦Holy Spirit, open my eyes and let me have a revelation vision of Christ in Jesus' name.

♦I command every hole or leak in my spiritual pipe to be sealed or closed now in the name of Jesus.

♦I destroy everything that is representing me in the demonic world with holy fire, burn up in the name of Jesus.

♦Let all those circulating my name for evil be disgraced in the name of Jesus.

♦I refuse to wear the garment of tribulation and sorrow.

♦The secrets of hidden and open enemies are revealed in the name of Jesus.

♦Holy Spirit, control my ability to frame my word.

♦Let the road close every unprofitable visitation in my life and church.

♦Let all evil friends make mistakes that would expose them in the name of Jesus.

♦O Lord let your favor and that of man encompass this year in the name of Jesus.

♦I cut down the roots of all problems in my life, spouse, and church.

◆Let every wicked house constructed against me, my family, and church die and burn now in the name of Jesus.

◆I declare with my mouth that nothing shall be impossible with me in the name of Jesus.

◆I will not lose my calling or ministry in the name of Jesus.

◆Lord put into my hand the gift that will elevate my calling in the name of Jesus.

◆I call every evil worm in any area of my life to die in the name of Jesus.

◆I command every blockage in my spiritual pipe to be cleared now in the name of Jesus Christ.

◆Holy Ghost, fill me that I might bring forth healing, deliverance, and power in the name of Jesus.

◆O Lord, remove me and my spouse from every root of irritation that keeps anger alive in the name of Jesus.

◆I bind every desert and all poverty spirits in my life and my spouse's life in the name of Jesus.

◆Every rebellion flees from my heart in the name of Jesus.

◆O Lord, renew a right spirit with me.

◆I will claim all my rights now in the name of Jesus.

◆O Lord, establish me as a holy person unto you Lord Jesus.

BREAKING POVERTY

Jesus is Lord of this earth. The earth with all its fullness belongs to God. As a joint heir with Jesus, I claim the wealth of this earth, for it belongs to Jesus.

♦I claim all that Jesus' death made available for me to receive, In Jesus' name.

♦I command you devil to loose the wealth of this earth! Take your hands off now!

♦I command every hindering force to stop!

♦In Jesus' name, Satan, I bind you and render you ineffective against me! I command wealth to come to me now! Jesus is Lord of my life. Jesus is Lord of my finances. Jesus is Lord!

♦I delight myself in the word of the Lord, therefore, I am blessed. Wealth and riches shall be in my house and my righteousness endures forever. Psalm 112:1-3

♦I remember the LORD my God: for it is he that gives me power to get wealth. Deuteronomy 8:18

♦With me are riches and honor, enduring wealth and prosperity. Proverbs 8:18

♦I am crowned with wealth. Proverbs 14:24

♦I know the grace of my Lord Jesus Christ, that, though He was rich, yet for my sake He became poor, that through His poverty, I might be rich. 2 Corinthians 8:9

♦I shout for joy and let the Lord be magnified, which hath pleasure in the prosperity of His servant. Psalm 35:27

♦The Lord is my Shepherd. Psalm 23:1

◆The Lord prepares a table before me in the presence of my enemies, He anoints my head with oil, and my cup runs over. Psalm 23:5

◆The blessing of the Lord makes me rich and He adds no trouble to it. Proverbs 10:22

◆I receive wealth from the Lord and the good health to enjoy it. Ecclesiastes 5:19

◆I am blessed because I trust in the Lord. I reverence the Lord, therefore there aren't any wants in my life. The young lions do lack and suffer hunger:

◆But I shall not want any good thing. Psalm 34:8-10.

◆I have given and it shall be given unto me, good measure, pressed down, shaken together and running over, shall men give into my bosom; For with the same measure that I mete withal it shall be measured to me again. Luke 6:38

◆God is able to make all grace abound toward me, that I, always having all sufficiency in all things, may have abundance for every good work. 2 Corinthians 9:8

◆I am prospering in every way. My body keeps well, even as my soul keeps well and prospers. 3 John 2

◆Whatsoever I ask the Father in the name of His son Jesus, He will give it to me. John 16:23

◆Abraham's blessings are mine. Galatians 6:9

◆Whatever I desire, when I pray, I believe that I have received them and I shall have them. Mark 11:24

◆I delight myself in the Lord, and He gives me the desires of my heart. Psalm 37:4

◆I seek first the kingdom of God; therefore everything I need shall be added unto me. Luke 12:31

◆The wealth of the sinner is laid up for me. Proverbs 13:22

◆My inheritance shall be forever. I shall not be ashamed in the evil time: and in the days of famine I shall be satisfied. Psalm 37:18-19

◆Every burden shall be taken away from off my shoulder, and every yoke from off my neck and the yoke shall be destroyed because of the anointing. Isaiah 10:27

◆I am like a tree that's planted by the rivers of water. Everything I do shall prosper. Psalm 1:3

◆I will not faint, for in due time and at the appointed season I shall reap, if I faint not. Galatians 6:9

FORGIVENESS

Mark 11:24-25 "Therefore I say to you, whatever things you ask when you pray, believe that you receive them, and you will have them. And whenever you stand praying, if you have anything against anyone, forgive him that your Father in heaven may also forgive you your trespasses."

For your word says that he in whom the Son sets free is free indeed. Father by the power of your spirit, I decree that I am set free from these and any other demonic spirits that would attempt to hold on to my mind, my heart, or my life in any way as a result of this transgression. I pray that you would also forgive me of all of my sins, transgressions, and iniquities.

Heavenly Father, as I have obeyed you and forgiven as according to your word; may none of my prayers be held back or hindered in any way in the name of Jesus. Now Heavenly Father, may you cause your open window blessing to be poured out upon me all the days of my life.

You instructed us to forgive those who wrong us and trespass against us. You also instructed us to pray for those who despitefully use us.

Heavenly Father, I ask that you would forgive _____, and release him/her from this transgression. Heavenly Father, I ask that the blessings of God be upon his/her life spiritually, physically, financially, and in every other aspect of his/her life.

Lord, allow me to truly forgive and release _____ in my heart. Heavenly Father, release me from the pain, hurt, discouragement, and disappointment this has caused in my life and in my heart. I thank you for filling that place with the love of God.

I bind the spirit of hatred, anger, strife, animosity, unforgiveness, bitterness, and any resentment that would try to hold on to my heart, as a result of this transgression and the power and authority of the hurt. In the name of Jesus Christ loose its grip and stronghold from my heart now.

RELEASING RESENTMENT AND BITTERNESS

"looking carefully lest anyone fall short of the grace of God; lest any root of bitterness springing up cause trouble, and by this many become defiled."--Hebrew 12:15

I choose to forgive those who have wronged me in the name of Jesus. I choose to live a life of forgiveness because you have forgiven me and I thank you Jesus. Devil I resist you, FLEE. I repent of all the resentments, bitterness, rage, anger, brawling, slander, and every form of malice in the name of Jesus.

The forgiveness of God is the foundation of every bridge from a hopeless past to a courageous present. I desire to be kind, loving, and compassionate to others, forgiving them, just as You forgave me. With the help of the Holy Spirit, I make every effort to live in peace with all men in Jesus' name.

I will not enter into temptation or cause others to stumble in Jesus name. I declare that I have overcome resentment and bitterness by the blood of the Lord Jesus Christ. Heavenly Father, I receive your anointing that breaks and destroys every yoke of bondage. I receive healing by faith according to your word.

I commit my life and all that is in it to you, to do your good works and to be in your total desire, will, and presence. I am and will be transformed into your total likeness in Jesus Christ's Holy name. Get behind me, Satan, for it is written "whom the son sets free is free indeed". I loose myself from every bind of Satan in the name of Jesus. (Luke 13:16).

Controlling Anger/ Developing A Good Attitude

Psalm 37:8
Cease from anger, and forsake wrath;
Do not fret—it only causes harm.

Ecclesiastes 7:9
Do not hasten in your spirit to be angry, for anger rests in the bosom of fools.

Proverbs 17:28
Even a fool is counted wise when he holds his peace; when he shuts his lips, he is considered perceptive.

Psalm 29:11
The Lord will give strength to His people; the Lord will bless His people with peace.

Psalm 34:13
Keep your tongue from evil,
And your lips from speaking deceit.

Daily Prayer Confessions

◆I overcome all because greater is He that is in me than he that is in the world. 1 John 4:4

◆I plead the blood of Jesus against every act of Satan in the name of Jesus.

⬩I am the head and not the tail. I am above not beneath in the name of Jesus. Deuteronomy 28:13

⬩I shall decree a thing and it shall be established in my life in the name of Jesus. Job 22:28

⬩I dwell in the secret place of the Most High and I abide under the shadow of the Almighty. Psalm 91:1

⬩I will be satisfied with long life and God will show me his salvation. Psalm 91:16

⬩Let me be satisfied with favor and filled with your blessing in the name of Jesus. Deuteronomy 33:23

⬩My children are taught of the Lord and great is their peace in the name of Jesus. Isaiah 54:13

⬩My seed is blessed in the name of Jesus. Psalm 37:26

⬩I command every evil plantation in my life, Come out with all your roots in the name of Jesus! **(Lay your hands on your stomach and keep repeating the emphasized area.)**

⬩Let every satanic noise scaring away my helpers be silenced, in the name of Jesus.

⬩I dismantle any power working against my efficiency, in Jesus name.

⬩My Heavenly Father, you are the God of harvest, let harvest meet harvest in my life daily, in the name of Jesus.

⬩Every good thing that I have lost from my mother's womb until today, I recover all now by holy fire in the name of Jesus!!!

Shout aloud five times

⬩I am rooted and grounded in love. Ephesians 3:17

⬩I have the love of Christ in my heart.

⬩I am planted by the rivers of water. Psalm 1:3

•I bring forth fruit in its season.

•My leaves shall not wither.
•Whatever I do shall prosper.

•I am the tree of righteousness and bear good fruit.

•My sins are forgiven and I am blessed.

•I break the enemy's bands (restraint) asunder and cast their cord (of control) from me in the name of Jesus. Psalms 2:3

•I will sing praise to your name, O most High, when my enemies turn back, they shall fall and perish at your presence. Psalm 9:2-3

•The spirit of the Lord, the spirit of wisdom, understanding, counsel, might, knowledge, and of the fear of the Lord shall rest upon me. Isaiah 11:2

•Lord this is my set time for favor. Psalm 102:13

•I am highly favored. Luke 1:28

•I am satisfied with favor and filled with your blessing. Deuteronomy 33:23

•Lord, you daily load me with benefits. Psalm 68:19

•I know you favor me because my enemies do not triumph over me. Psalm 41:11

•Let your words have free course in my life. 2 Thessalonians 3:1

•I loose me from the bands of wickedness. Isaiah 58:6

•My breakthrough is not negotiable, I move forward by the Holy Ghost in Jesus' name.

•I am righteous and shall flourish like the palm tree; I shall grow like a cedar in Lebanon.

♦Satan is destroyed from morning to evening: They perish forever without any regarding it. The stronghold of the mighty can be destroyed at midnight.

♦I overcame Satan by the Blood of the Lamb and by the word of my testimony.

♦In Him I have redemption through His Blood, the forgiveness of sin according to the riches of His grace.

♦I call on the name above all names, Jesus, he is my help.

♦Whatsoever I shall ask the Father in His name, He will give it to me. John 16:33.

♦I will bring forth fruit that should remain. John 15:16.

♦In the name of Jesus Christ of Nazareth, rise up and walk. Acts 3.

Paralyzing any Evil Hands

As you embark on this prayer program, all evil hands in your life will be paralyzed. The works that they have used their hands to do against you will begin to work against them. It's these evil hands that form evil weapons against God's children. Thank God that their weapons cannot prosper against our lives.

Psalm 140:4
Keep me, O Lord, from the hands of the wicked; preserve me from violent men, who have purposed to make my steps stumble.

Psalm 9:1
The Lord is known by the judgment He executes; the wicked is snared in the work of his own hands.

Psalm 115:4
Their idols are silver and gold,
The work of men's hands.

REVELATION
STEPPING INTO THE POWER
SOURCE THROUGH REVELATION

◆Let the hidden things be made manifest. Mark 4:22.

◆Let me know and understand the mysteries of the kingdom.

◆Let me receive and understand your hidden wisdom. 1 Corinthians 2:7

◆Open my eyes to behold wondrous things in your word. Psalm 119:18

◆Let me understand the deep things of God. 1 Corinthians 2:10.

◆Let my reins instruct me in the night season and let me awaken with revelation. Psalm 16:7.

◆Heavenly Father, give me the treasures of darkness and hidden riches in the secret place. Isaiah 45:3

◆Lord, reveal to me the secret and deep things. Daniel 2:22.

Lay your hand on yourself and pray three times daily.

Ephesians 1:17-19 "that the God of our Lord Jesus Christ, the Father of glory, may give to you the spirit of wisdom and revelation in the knowledge of Him, the eyes of your understanding being enlightened; that you may know what is the hope of His calling, what are the riches of the glory of His inheritance in the saints, and what is the exceeding greatness of His power toward us who believe, according to the working of His mighty power.

POWER OVER DEATH

1 Corinthians 15:55
"O Death, where is your sting?
O Hades, where is your victory?"

Hebrews 5:7
"During the days of Jesus' life on earth, he offered up prayers and petitions with loud cries and tears to the one who could save him from death, and he was heard because of his reverent submission" NIV

Psalm 118:17
"I will not die but live, and proclaim what the Lord has done" NIV

Psalm 91:16
"With long life I will satisfy him and show him my salvation" NIV

Death was defeated the day Jesus rose from the dead. Resurrection morning marked the defeat of the devil. I shall not die but live and declare the works of God. God has promised that he will satisfy us with long life.

I break and loose myself from any spiritual agreement that the devil set for death. Satan you won't use my life for promotion. I close every door opened to Satan that will bring death and I break and loose myself and my loved ones from every dark spirit and satanic bondage that brings death to my life. I call every poison comes out of my life and my body now.

Lord, drain sickness and worry out of my life. I destroy all secret power sources that hinder. Every tentacle and root of death, I tear it down and destroy the hidden works of the enemy. Rebuke the spirit of death using these prayer points and fulfill the number of your days. Pray these prayers and you shall have the last laugh and God will perfect that which concerns you.

•Let my prayer alters receive power today in the name of Jesus.

•Lord let your glory be manifested in my life in the name of Jesus.

•I break and loose myself from any curse, bewitching, witchcraft, and charm put upon my life and the lives of my family, in the name of Jesus.

•I overthrow and release myself from evil demonic control in the name of Jesus.

•I break any evil stronghold of death over my life and my spouse's life.

•Every power, speaking impossibility into my present unfavorable situation, fall down and die from the root in the name of Jesus.

•Blood of Jesus flush out and scatter witchcraft meetings, summoned for my sake. I seal the rebuke with the blood.

•I bind and cast out any spirit executing evil curses against me in the name of Jesus.

•Let the blood of Jesus rub off evil ointment upon my head I call upon my body goodness in the name of Jesus.

•Every visible and invisible alter, I sentence it to confusion and trouble all year in the name of Jesus.

•Let the river of cancer from my family line that's flowing into my life dry up from the roots and never return in the name of Jesus.

•I speak failure into every satanic weapon formed against my life, my spouse's life and my children in the name of Jesus.

♦Every agent of health destruction working in my life fall and die now by the blood of Jesus.

♦I speak frustration into every evil snare and satanic pit fashioned against my family, my church, and my life in the name of Jesus.

♦Let favor meet favor in my life and be increased mightily in the name of Jesus.

♦I terminate every evil progress of death in every area of my life in the name of Jesus.

♦I will become all that God created me to be in the name of Jesus.

♦I cancel reports brought against me and my spouse in the kingdom of darkness in the name of Jesus.

♦I revoke and nullify every judgment passed upon me in the kingdom of darkness in the name of Jesus.

♦I abort the operation and assignment of the power of darkness commissioned against my name, my family, and my church in the name of Jesus.

EXERCISING FAITH FOR YOUR HEALING

When you have faith that you will be healed, you draw out the healing power of God. His power is released on your behalf. When the healing virtue (anointing) is present, we can use our faith to put a demand on that anointing; then it will be released unto you.

Shout this scripture out before God. Make Satan tremble

Psalm 103:1-5 (AMP)

¹BLESS (AFFECTIONATELY, gratefully praise) the Lord, O my soul; and all that is [deepest] within me, bless His holy name! ²Bless (affectionately, gratefully praise) the Lord, O my soul, and forget not [one of] all His benefits- ³Who forgives [every one of] all your iniquities, Who heals [each one of] all your diseases, ⁴Who redeems your life from the pit and corruption, Who beautifies, dignifies, and crowns you with loving-kindness and tender mercy; ⁵Who satisfies your mouth [your necessity and desire at your personal age and situation] with good so that your youth, renewed, is like the eagle's [strong, overcoming, soaring]!

Psalm 107:20 (NIV)

He sent out his word and healed them; he rescued them from the grave.

ACTIVATING YOUR HEALTH

♦Heavenly Father, I pray that you forgive me of my sins and iniquities in Jesus' name.

♦I believe God for healing miracles in my life and my family's lives in Jesus' name.

♦I break every curse of infirmity, sickness, and premature death off of my body. Every hidden sickness and every hidden disease, I command you to leave my body in the name of Jesus.

•In the name of Jesus, I speak to every sickness that attempts to live in my body. Dry up and die now. I plead blood of Jesus against Satan, in the name of Jesus.

•I command kidney, lung, back, liver problems be removed now in Jesus name.

•Galatians 3:13 flows through every tissue of my body in the name of Jesus.

•I command all sickness and disease to die from the root in the name of Jesus.

•All joint conditions and pain must go now by the power of the blood of Jesus.

•I speak to all hidden infections to come out of my body in the name of Jesus.

•I break any and all addictions (food, drug, pain pills, etc.) in the name of Jesus.

•I am the temple of the Holy Spirit. Therefore all heart and circulatory conditions, irregular heartbeat, angina, and stroke must leave my body, go in the name of Jesus.

•I decree, tumors die from the root now in the name of Jesus. Isaiah 53:5 that states "But He was wounded for our transgressions, He was bruised for our iniquities; the chastisement for our peace was upon Him, and by His stripes we are healed." I am healed now through the blood of Jesus.

•Every hidden disease I command you to leave this body in Jesus name.

•I speak to blood and skeletal conditions, be made whole now in Jesus' name.

•I speak to diabetes, high blood pressure, cancer, multiple sclerosis, and stroke, GO, I cast you out of my body in the name of Jesus.

•My body is whole and sound; no sickness can live in this body in Jesus' name.

•Growth and tumors have no right to my body. They are a thing of the past for I am delivered from the authority of darkness by the blood of Jesus Christ.

•Every organ and tissue of my body functions in order and in the perfection that God created it. I forbid any malfunction in my body in Jesus name.

•Jesus took my infirmities and bore my sickness. Therefore I refuse to allow sickness to dominate my body. Matthew 8:17

•The life of God flows within me bringing healing to every fiber of my being.

•God's word is manifested in my body, causing growths to disappear. Arthritis and blood pressure issues are a thing of the past. I make demands on my blood levels. My bones and joints function properly in the name of Jesus.

Seed faith: when you plant a seed, God changes the nature of that seed so that it becomes a plant and the power of life surges in that tender, young plant to such a great extent that even a mountain of earth cannot stop it from pushing upward! Jesus said our faith in God is like a seed. When we release it to God, it takes on a totally new nature. It takes in the nature of a miracle in the making. Nothing will be impossible for you.

•You have given me abundant life; I receive that life through your word. Life, flow to every organ of my body and bring healing and health. According to John 10:10, Jesus came that we may have life and have it to full. God gives longevity.

•I am redeemed from the curse.

•The Word flows to every cell and fiber of my body restoring life and health.

◆All of my afflictions will leave and not come back again in the name of Jesus.

◆I command every T cell of my body to be normal in the name of Jesus. Every disease, germ, and virus that tried to inhabit my body is destroyed now in the name of Jesus.

◆I demand my body to release the right chemicals and have the accurate chemical balance. My pancreas secretes the proper amount of insulin for life and health.

◆I am alive and well. By His stripes I am healed and made whole. God is watching over his word to perform it.

Shout aloud-Sickness and disease have no power over me; I am forgiven and free from all sin and guilt. I am dead to sin and alive to righteousness. Amen.

Five Day Prayer

I will speak with wisdom and promote health. I declare that I am in good health, I am alive. The healing of the Lord will spring forth speedily

I declare that I prosper in all things, am in good health, just as my soul prospers. 1 Peter 2:24 says that I am healed

How you can be healed

He has made healing available to you through many avenues. They are:

1. Healing through prayer. Matthew 21:22, James 5:16
2. Healing through virtue or touch. Mark 5:29-30, Luke 6:19
3. Healing through the presence of God. Luke 5:17
4. Healing through cloths. Acts 19:12
5. Healing through anointing oil. Mark 6:13
6. Healing through faith. Mark 11:23

7. Healing through deliverance. Matt 8:16

God's healing is available to all. Jesus heals all sicknesses. You must expect to be healed. Sicknesses and diseases are works of the devil. According to Colossians 2:15, Jesus came and disarmed principalities and powers. He made a public spectacle of them, triumphing over them. Healing belongs to you!!!
Shout 10 times

I AM HEALED!!!!

BREAKING CURSES

◆I break all spoken curses and negative words that I have spoken over my life in the name of Jesus.

◆I break the legal rights of all generational spirits operating behind a curse in the name of Jesus.

◆Satan, you have no legal right to operate in my life. I bind you now and cast into dry places in the name of Jesus.

Declaration; I break the curse of alcohol and drugs. Satan you and your evil spirits of alcoholism have no more rights to neither my life nor my family's lives. Your power is broken in the name of Jesus.

◆I break the curse. Spirits of spiders, scorpions, lizards, vultures, bats, snakes, turtles, frogs, and hornets in my life I cast them out of my life and church family.
Through the finished work of Jesus Christ I have authority to declare that the generational curses in my family are broken

♦I break generational curses of divorce, adultery, rebellion, sterility, and debt.

♦I break and root out the curse, way down deep, iniquities, and seed in soil of my soul, mind, will, and emotions in the name of Jesus.

♦I root out every anger and health problem.

♦I decree that I am free from every generational curse; I am breaking the pattern once and for all. The problem is solved in Jesus' name.

♦I release the spirit of bitterness from my life. I decree the curse of depression be broken in the name of Jesus.

♦I ask your forgiveness and cleansing through the blood of the Lord Jesus Christ according to I John 4:14.

♦Heavenly Father, I have repented of all of my sins and I thank you for forgiving me in the name of Jesus.

♦I now ask you to destroy all generational curses that have been placed on me, my spouse, and my children including ten generations in Jesus' name Amen!

SPIRITUAL WARFARE [BONDAGE BREAKING]

♦I bind all of Satan's evil, wicked, demonic, lying, and tormenting spirits in the name of the Lord Jesus Christ of Nazareth. I loose the peace of God over my life.

◆I bind the strongmen along with all their works, root, fruits, tentacles, and links of abuse, abandonment, defeatism, deafness, divination, belittling, anguish, animosity, apathy, confusion, occultism, covetousness, bickering, black magic, confrontation, non-submissiveness, and complaining in the name of Jesus.

◆I break and cast down self-centeredness, rape, lust of the eyes, lust of the flesh, incest, frustration, heaviness, and hopelessness in the name of Jesus. I command the blood line around my life.

◆I pray that I will now be set completely free from anything that now binds me, cancer, tumors, arthritis, forgetfulness, and all spirits of disorders and disease.

◆I loose the strongman out of his place now, along with all evil principalities, powers, and rulers of wickedness in high places from every organ, cell, gland, in my body.

◆I loose them to go where Jesus sends them---into a dry place and never return in Jesus name. I bind them to stay there in the name of Jesus Christ of Nazareth.

◆Heavenly Father, I ask you to cause your anointing to break and destroy every yoke of bondage in my life.

◆In the name of the Lord Jesus Christ, I bind the strongman that may spoil his house, taking back every bit of joy, peace, blessing, freedom, and every material and spiritual possession that Satan has stolen from me, I take them back right now.

◆I loose the strongman's influence over every part of my (our) body, soul, and spirit in Jesus name.

◆I loose, crush, smash, and destroy every evil device the enemy may try to bring into their sphere of influence during this day. I loose these things in Jesus' holy name. He has given me the keys and authority to do so!

•In the name of the Lord Jesus Christ of Nazareth, I bind all satanic spirits of sorcery, Ahab, Herod, Python, mind-binding, and mind-blocking spirits in the name of Jesus.

•I apply the precious blood of the Lord Jesus Christ, from the tops of my (our) head to the sole of my (our) feet.

•I plead the blood of Jesus over my marriage, businesses, finances, and ministries.

•I plead the blood of Jesus. I cancel the power of any evil spirit and render it powerless in Jesus' name.

•Heavenly Father, I thank you for your mighty work. Grant me the grace, power, and desire to be persistent in my intercession for others and myself that you may be glorified through our deliverance in Jesus name Amen.

BE HEALED

•O Sun of Righteousness! Arise and heal my body, marriage, career, destiny, infirmity, [mention whatever you need the touch of God for] in the name of Jesus.

•Every gate of sorrow and failure is uprooted and consumed by Jehovah's furnace in the name of Jesus.

•I break free from every prison of Satan programmed against my destiny, in the name of Jesus.

•I commend every power assigned against my health, die, your cycle shall never be completed in the name of Jesus.

Psalm 56:9, "When I cry to you, then shall my enemies turn back: this I know; for God is for me."

♦Every siege and invasion of diseases and infirmity on my life and my family; I send you back to sender that release you, by the blood of Jesus!

♦The transgressions and iniquities, blocking my healing, I drag you under the blood of Jesus, you will never return to my body again, in the Jesus of name!

Psalm 56:8, "You keep track of all my sorrows. You have collected all my tears in your bottle. You have recorded each one in your book."

Hosea 6:1, "Come, let us return to the Lord for He has torn us, but He will heal us; He has wounded us, but He will bandage us."

Psalm 41:4, "As for me, I said O Lord be gracious to me; Heal my soul, for I have sinned against you.

Psalm 30:2, "O Lord my God, I cried to you for help, and you restored my health."

Put your hand on your head (Shout loudly)

♦Every arrow of sickness fired against my body, my soul, and my spirit I decree seven-fold return on my healing in Jesus' name.

♦Satan the blood of Jesus is against you; loose my health now, in Jesus name.

♦Everything purchased by the blood of Jesus and that is still missing in my life I declare it to come forth, in Jesus' name!

♦Everything that Jesus my Lord died for to make me free and partake of all blessings, I call it to manifest now, in the name of Jesus.

•O Lord my God, let my tears of pain trigger your vengeance against every infirmity and their sponsors, in the name of Jesus. Psalm 6:2, "Be merciful to me, Lord, for I am faint; O Lord heal me, for my bones are in agony.

Covenant Healing

I will bless the Lord, O my soul.

I will not forget all of my benefits. You forgive all of my iniquities and heal all my diseases. I thank you for redeeming my life from destruction, and crowning me with loving kindness and tender mercies. You satisfy my mouth with good things, so that my youth is renewed like the eagle.

No weapon formed against me shall prosper,
This is the heritage of the servants of the Lord,
I shall be like a tree planted by the rivers of water, but whatever I do will prosper.

THE JEHOVAH NAMES IN THE OLD TESTAMENT

EL ROI: The God who sees me. Genesis 16:13

ELOHIM: my creator Genesis 1:1

JEHOVAH: The Lord Exodus 6:2-3

JEHOVAH SHAMMAH: The Lord is there Ezekiel 48:35

EL SHADDAI: My supplier Genesis 18:3

ADONAI: My master and Lord Genesis 18:3

JEHOVAH JIREH: My provider Genesis 22:14

JEHOVAH ROPHE: The Lord that heals. Exodus 15:26

JEHOVAH NISSI: My banner and victory. Exodus 17:15

JEHOVAH KABODHI: The Lord my glory. Psalm 3:3

JEHOVAH MIKKADES: My sanctifier. Leviticus 20:7-8

JEHOVAH T SIDKENU: My righteousness. Jeremiah 23:5-6

JEHOVAH SHALOM: The Lord my peace. Judges 6:24

JEHOVAH ROHI: The Lord my shepherd Psalm 23:1

JEHOVAH TSUR: O Lord my Rock   Psalm 28:1

JEHOVAH SABAOTH: The Lord of hosts Psalm 24:10

JEHOVAH ORI: The Lord my Light Psalm 27:1

JEHOVAH ELYON: The name of the Lord most high Psalm 7:17

JEHOVAH MELECH 'OLAM: The Lord is king forever Psalm 10:16

THE ETERNAL GOD Deuteronomy 33:27

EL GIBBOR: the almighty God Jeremiah 32:18

EL KHAY: The Living God Joshua 3:10

JEHOVAH GO'EL: The Lord thy Redeemer Isaiah 49:26, 60:16

JEHOVAH ELI: The Lord my God Psalm 18:2

It is very important to understand the Jehovah names of the Holy Spirit and how they can help you know God more intimately. As you learn about His many names, you will find yourself entering into a deeper, richer, and more joyous relationship with God.

PRAYER FOR YOUTH

◆I command every shackle and chain tied to young men/women, that brings darkness, are broken. I put gaps in your assignment now in the name of Jesus.

◆I break every form of demonic influence through money, sex, and drugs. I loose the authority that you have over the lives of young men and women in the name of Jesus.

◆He/She has been redeemed through the blood of Jesus.

◆The strongmen have been overcome by the blood of the Lamb and the word of God.

◆I bind the demonic power of influence from our young people.

◆I cast down all ungodly soul ties, satanic oaths, and blood sacrifices to the place where God sends it. It will never return again.

◦All things have become new in and on_____ life. I pronounce that he/she has the mind of Christ, in Jesus' name.

◆Old things have become new, new wine in a new wine skin in his/her life. He /She press toward the mark of Jesus Christ.

◆The spirit of disobedience and rebellion are under arrest, by the Holy Spirit. Hallelujah! Praise the Lord. _____ hears God's voice now and all vicious cycles are broken in the name of Jesus.

◆Every reoccurring spirit is shut down, catch on fire in Jesus name.

♦Heavenly Father, I ask you to destroy all demonic covenants, contracts, chains, fetters, bondages, and captivities that are contrary to oppose or hinder your will and destiny for his/her live, in Jesus' name.

♦Heavenly Father, I decree that every assignment over the lives of youths who are in gangs, addicted, or are on the streets is broken. I decree the hedges of protection around them in the name of Jesus.

♦I forbid evil from sucking their soul into hell, in the name of Jesus.

♦Let the prisoner suicide be loosed from his or her life, now in the name of Jesus.

♦Loose those appointed to death and call forth life in that daughter/son, in the name of Jesus.

♦I loose the death angel from his assignment over our city and regions.

♦I release shame upon the enemy.

♦Heavenly Father let not the enemy persecute his/her soul in the name of Jesus.

♦I command the soul of his/her that are haunted by the enemy to go in the Jesus name.

♦I break the power of all negative words spoken against his/her soul be reversed and sent back to the sender, in the name of Jesus.

♦He/She shall have no more struggles to overcome the devil. He/she walks an overcomer's life in Christ Jesus. Angelic armies of Heaven strategize in warfare for him/her and root out the forces of darkness in the name of Jesus.

♦I bind and cast out any creeping, demonic spirit that would attempt to creep into his/her life in Jesus' name.

♦I bind and cast out all spirits of self-deception in the name of Jesus.

♦I command every ungodly generational trap root to be cut and pulled out of that young boy/girl's blood line, in the name of Jesus.

♦I release and declare that every root of bitterness be cut from this young person's life in Jesus' name.

♦Heavenly Father let this young girl/boy be clothed with humility.

♦Heavenly Father, cover them with the robe of righteousness.

♦Father let your mantle of power rest upon their head.

♦Lord Jesus let no man deceive him/her with lies.

♦Heavenly Father, I pray for boldness and utterance to make known the mystery of the gospel to young boys and girls by the Holy Ghost.

♦Let them increase and abound in love.

♦O Lord, increase his/her knowledge in school.

♦Lord let his/her latter end greatly increase.

♦He/She has redemption in Christ Jesus.

♦They will flourish like a palm tree and grow like a cedar in Lebanon.

♦Lord you said you will give them double for their shame.
Isaiah 61:7 states "Instead of your shame you shall have double honor, And instead of confusion they shall rejoice in their portion. Therefore in their land they shall possess double; Everlasting joy shall be theirs."

Uprooting The Root Of Non-Achievement

Matthew 3:10, "And even now the ax is laid to the root of the trees.

Therefore every tree which does not bear good fruit is cut down and thrown into the fire."

God is ready to help you. God is not the author of failure! Everything God created was good according to Genesis chapter one. God is ready to assist you in order to uproot every tree of non-achievement such as profitless, fruitless effort, constant frustrations, and failure in achieving anything in life, finance coffins, satanic embargos on progress, tortoise and snail anointing, and sluggish progress.

This prayer is for those who have been fishing, catching nothing, in the ocean of life. Also, for those who observe that there is little or nothing to show for living. We cannot reflect His glory in lack and poverty.

Ephesians 2:10, "For we are His workmanship, created in Christ Jesus for good works, which God prepared beforehand that we should walk in them."

Galatians 3:13-14
[13] "Christ has redeemed us from the curse of the law, having become a curse for us (for it is written, "Cursed is everyone who hangs on a tree), [14] that the blessing of Abraham might come upon the Gentiles in Christ Jesus, that we might receive the promise of the Spirit through faith."

Psalm 27:2

"When the wicked came against me to eat up my flesh, my enemies and foes, they stumbled and fell."

Confession

♦Let the fire of God destroy every power, operating any spiritual vehicle, working against me.

♦I command all demonic reverse gears, installed to hinder my progress, die now in the name of Jesus.

♦I command all foundational strongmen, attached to my life or my spouse, to be paralyzed in the name of Jesus.

♦I release myself/spouse/child from inherited bondage.

♦Let every gate opened to the enemy by my foundation or my business be closed forever with the blood of Jesus.

♦I release me from the grip of any problems transferred into my life from the womb.

♦I break and loose myself from every form of demonic bewitching.

♦Let the blood of Jesus flush every inherited satanic deposit out of my system.

♦Let the wind, the sun, and the moon run contrary to every demonic presence in my environment in the name of Jesus.

♦Let any evil tongue that is against me roast in fire in the name of Jesus.

♦Let all satanic manipulation, aimed at changing my destiny, be frustrated in the name of Jesus.

♦Let every spirit of Sanballat and Tobiah planning evil against me receive the stones of fire in the name of Jesus.

♦Let every spirit of evil be disgraced in the name of Jesus.

◆Let every evil effect of any strange touches be removed from my life, in the name of Jesus.

◆Every destructive plan of the enemy aimed against me; blow up now, in the name of Jesus.

◆I break and loose myself from every inherited evil curse in the name of Jesus.

◆You evil foundation and plantations come out of my life with all your roots, in Jesus' name.

◆O, you devourers, vanish from my labor in the name of Jesus.

◆All powers sponsoring evil decisions against me falls down and are disgraced, in the name of Jesus.

◆Every spirit of Pharaoh falls into the Red Sea of its own making in the name of Jesus.

Thank God for making the provision for deliverance from any form of bondage.

◆Every evil imagination against me withers from the source in the name of Jesus.

◆God's make cannot be spoiled or ruined in the name of Jesus.

II Timothy 4:18
And the Lord will deliver me from every evil work and preserve me for His heavenly kingdom. To Him be glory forever and ever. Amen!

Colossians 2:15
Having disarmed principalities and powers, He made a public spectacle of them, triumphing over them in it.

BREAKTHROUGH WATCH

The twilight zone is the hours of confrontation between heavenly host and force of darkness. It is a time for uncommon angelic traffic.

A day that the kingdoms of darkness seek to lay evil foundations for persons, place, and things.

There are days marked out for specific spiritual transactions. Satan and his agents always seek to hijack days to pervert God's plans and purpose.

In the twilight zone, there is of intensive warfare between darkness and light.

It is a time for laying new spiritual foundation to take hold of the future; and a day of conflict between the children of God and strongman of darkness.

Psalm 2

♦Every beast of the earth assigned to torment me this year, die in the name of Jesus.

♦My Father, release violent earthquakes to destroy every satanic barrier that hinders my progress in Jesus name.

♦Every satanic priest sustaining evil alters in this country; die in the name of Jesus.

♦I decree that every occultist power troubling this nation; will have darkness without divination in the name of Jesus.

♦I decree that every evil man boasting with satanic powers; will grope in the day like blind men in the dark, in the name of Jesus.

◆I decree that the sun will set upon every satanic priest and prophet that cause trouble to this nation in Jesus' name.

◆I take charge of the heavenlies and declare that it shall be well with me in the name of Jesus.

◆We command the heavens not to respond to the voices of spiritualists and occultists in the name of Jesus.

◆Every priest of darkness monitoring my destiny, dry up, in the name of Jesus name.

◆Lord Jesus, we ask you to destroy any familiar spirit that has allowed these demonic strongmen into our presence.

◆I declare, in the name of Jesus, that all of Satan's works, roots, fruit, tentacles, and links are now dead works in my life. I declare that all demonic power over me is broken in Jesus' name.

◆Heavenly Father, I bow, I worship, and I praise you. I apply the blood of Jesus over myself, my church, my family, and over the air that surrounds us.

TWILIGHT ANOINTING FINANCE

21 Day Prayer

Pray this during the day and midnight, cover it with a 12 hour fast (12 midnight to 12 noon), or you can go further till 6:00 pm. If you have the grace, I know that by the assurance of faith in the awesome power of God is that you will not come out of this encounter the same way you entered it in Jesus' name.

Matthew 12:29

"How can anyone enter a strong man's house and carry off his possessions unless he first ties up the strong man?"

Confession

◆I curse every demonic spirit recurring over my finances. I send it into a desert place.

◆Every satanic mouth assigned to devour my promotions and breakthroughs; I shut you up by fire of the Holy Spirit in the name of Jesus.

◆I will arise and go forth in the name of Jesus.

◆I activate every promise of God, concerning my life, with effectual prayers that brings unstoppable performance.

◆Anything in my life that is presently limiting God's move, burn up now in the name of Jesus.

◆Blood of Jesus, speak against ancient doors of poverty in my business' foundation, in Jesus' name.

◆The powers that give up when miracles are around me; I command that power to die now in the name of Jesus.

◆Let my business and my church bring forth prosperity in the name of Jesus.

◆I declare that Satan will have no control over my finances, in Jesus name.

◆Let the ministering spirit (God's Angles) go forth. Bring blessings unto me in the name of Jesus.

◆I take charge of the heavens and I declare that is shall be well with me, in the name of Jesus.

◆Let there be no agreement in the strongman's house.

Destroying The Throne Of Witchcraft

♦Heavenly Father, every witchcraft throne hiding in the body of Christ, be revealed. Let the ground open and swallow it up in the name of Jesus.

♦I cast down every stronghold of flying thrones of witchcraft, in the name of Jesus.

♦Let the Throne of Jesus Christ be established in every area of my life, in the name of Jesus.

♦Let the thunder of God locate and dismantle the throne of witchcraft in my household.

♦Every throne of witchcraft in my neighborhood, be pulled down and die in the name of Jesus.

♦I drive out and dismantle witchcraft embargos on finances.

♦I recover all my finances from witchcraft embargoes in the name of Jesus.

♦Every ancestral embargo on my finances, break, fall, and die in the name of Jesus.

♦Anything in me supporting witchcraft embargo on my finances come out with all your roots and tentacles, in the name of Jesus Christ.

♦O Heavenly Father, every witchcraft eye manipulating my finances be plucked off, in the name of Jesus.

♦I declare that every witchcraft eye manipulating my body and my spiritual life is cut off, by an arrow of fire, in the name of Jesus.

◆I bind the eyes of envious witchcraft monitoring my life, in the name of Jesus Christ.

◆I break all demonic witchcraft spirit from over and around my children and grandchildren; be confused and die in Jesus' name.

Destroying the Covens of Witchcraft

◆O Lord, let your thunder and fire locate all covens of witches and wizards established against me for total destruction by the Blood of Jesus.

◆I cast down all witchcraft banks and strong room harboring my blessing and treasures be pull down by fire burn in the name of Jesus.

◆Every area of my life caged by witchcraft coven be broken and released now by fire in the name Jesus.

◆I decree that all witchcraft covens, that are calling my name for evil, be cast down and destroyed by fire in the name of Jesus.

Communication Systems of Witchcraft

◆Let the communication of witches be frustrated. No agreement or connection concerns my household and my church in name of Jesus.

◆Every witchcraft network working against my church, my community, and my prosperity be dismantled by fire. I decree no connection, no agreement in his camp, in the name of Jesus.

◆Heavenly Father, let every computer assigned witchcraft against my life, my family's lives, and my church, be destroyed by Holy fire, dismantling the communication, in the name of Jesus.

◆O Heavenly Father, confuse every witchcraft tongue speaking against my destiny and the destiny of my family, in the name of Jesus.

◆I break every evil communication against me, my family, and my church. It falls down and dies now in the name of Jesus.

◆I decree good communication of God and the Holy Spirit to my life.

Power against Witchcraft Burial

◆I declare, in the name of Jesus, that the power of witchcraft burial against my finances be reversed now in your name. I call all of my prosperity forth.

◆O Lord, let the power of witchcraft burial against my family and my prayers be nullified in the name of Jesus.
(Remember, God said you decree a thing is will be establish lay your right hand on your head)

◆I call all blessings and health imprisoned by the grave to come forth in the name of Jesus.

◆I release my blessings, my healing, and my soul from the hand of dead relations in the name of Jesus.

◆I withdraw my blessing from the hand of any dead and demonic relation, in the name of Jesus.

◆Whatever has been done against me using the ground or underground, I dismiss it and call it to be neutralized now in the name of Jesus. Dry up from the root and die, I apply the Blood of Jesus on it now.

◆Every witchcraft burial against the covenant of my marriage is reversed now. I call my marriage whole and sound now in the name of Jesus.

◆I rout out and overthrow the power of darkness. All are defeated demons; I send them into dry places. They will never return to my house, my body, or my family. Glory Hallelujah! Praise God!

I decree that every prayer that has been prayed will be answered by the Holy God and Satan will be confused. I apply the Blood of Jesus over my life, family, and my church. Hallelujah!!!

Prayers To Bring Peace

"God is in the middle of her; she shall not be moved: God shall help her and that right early."

"The heathen raged, the kingdoms were moved: he uttered his voice, the earth melted."

"The LORD of hosts is with us; the God of Jacob is our refuge. Selah."

"Come; behold the works of the LORD, what desolations he has made in the earth."

"He makes wars to cease to the end of the earth; he breaks the bow, and cuts the spear in sunder; he burns the chariot in the fire."

"Be still, and know that I am God: I will be exalted among the heathen, I will be exalted in the earth."

The LORD of hosts is with us; the God of Jacob is our refuge." Psalms 46:6-11

◆Rivers of joy and gladness flow through my soul today and every day in Jesus' name.

•Every power delegated to move me from joy to sorrow and from peace to strife; your mission is a failure. Release me and die in the name of Jesus.

•Every Mountain of trouble and strife standing before me, I challenge you by fire. Become prey to the consuming fire of God in Jesus' name.

•Speedy divine intervention, appear and rescue me from every trouble and strife of tongues in Jesus' name.

•Every rage of dark kingdoms against my peace and family, melt away by fire in Jesus 'name.

•Every spear thrown at me and my family to cause agony, I break and multiply you into seven fiery inescapable arrows of vengeance. Go and kill your owner in Jesus' name.

•Every chariot of trouble assigned against me, I cast you into tribulations now in the name of Jesus.

•O men of war, strengthen my inner man to overcome and triumph over strife targeted at me in Jesus' name.

•Every hatred of the heathen for me is melted by the Holy Ghost's fire in Jesus' name.

•O my God, let my enemies know that you are God in my life. Be exalted in earth; be exalted among the heathen in Jesus' name.

•O God of Jacob, fight for me and fight my battles now in the name of Jesus.

•O God of Abraham, Isaac, and Jacob, arise and surround me and my family as our refuge in the name of Jesus.

•Holy Spirit, even in the midst of tumult, let me hear your still, small voice for comfort and direction in the name of Jesus.

Scriptures

Psalm 46:1-7
"God is our refuge and strength, a very present help in trouble. Therefore will not we fear, though the earth be removed, and though the mountains be carried into the middle of the sea; Though the waters thereof roar and be troubled, though the mountains shake with the swelling thereof. Selah.

There is a river, the streams whereof shall make glad the city of God, the holy place of the tabernacles of the most High. God is in the middle of her; she shall not be moved: God shall help her, and that right early. The heathen raged, the kingdoms were moved: he uttered his voice, the earth melted. The LORD of hosts is with us; the God of Jacob is our refuge. Selah. Come; behold the works of the LORD, what desolations he has made in the earth."

Philippians 4:6-7
"Be anxious for nothing, but in everything by prayer and supplication, with thanksgiving, let your requests be made known unto God; and the peace of god, which passes all understanding, will guard your hearts and minds through Christ Jesus."

Romans 5:1
Therefore, having been justified by faith, we have peace with God through our Lord Jesus Christ.

John 14:27
Peace I leave with you, My peace I give to you: not as the world gives do I give to you. Let not your heart be troubled, neither let it be afraid."

Romans 8:6
"For to be carnally minded is death, but to be spiritually minded is life and peace.

Isaiah 26:3

"You will keep him in perfect peace, whose mind is stayed on You, because he trusts in You."

CPSIA information can be obtained at www.ICGtesting.com
Printed in the USA
BVOW032238071112

304972BV00001B/64/P